# I COLOR
## ADULTS COLORING BOOK

Illustrated & Created by:

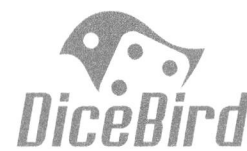

Colour therapy is a growing trend among adults, both young and old, everything from the very simple to complex designs are being put out there, and it is taking off everywhere ! It is used in many countries. This is one method that professionals are using in the treatment of many illnesses and for therapy, Anxiety, depression, chronic pain such as 'fibromyalgia' and other chronic pain sufferers, it has amazing therapeutic value, this is a great way to relieve stress and help take your mind off of everything and focus on creating, it is also being used on stroke victims to help teach hand and eye coordination, movement and recognition.

Mandalas are among some of the most common designs; many of them have meanings behind them. They are also among some of the most relaxing and beautiful designs out there.

DICEBIRD has created several for you to enjoy, they range from floral to crystal like and go from fairly easy to very complex, you can see his passion for art in each of his drawings, and his love of people has made him want to create so that they may enjoy.

There is no right or wrong way to color, as a matter of fact there are many !
Below are a few examples of the ways i choose colors, it depends on my mindset, my pain level, the amount of time I have and of course the drawing.

- Colour Schemes
- Varying shades of one color
- Just pick a colour randomly or close my eyes and pick. ( This is fun and often turns out extremely well )

Find a nice, peaceful, relaxing place such as a flower garden or a park or even just simply sitting in your own home or yard, nowadays it is not unheard of to take your supplies to work and colour when on break or on a long trip, take a picnic lunch or just something to drink and perhaps a snack, set your supplies up and begin. Breathe deeply and let yourself get into what you are doing, and let your worries drift away as you get farther into your piece, it helps to choose your picture and colours beforehand but is absolutely not necessary !

You don't have to be an artist; you just need to know how to use a pen, pencil, marker or crayon. You are only limited by your imagination ! If you want a purple cow or perhaps a pink moon then by all means, go for it, the tricks will come with time and experience.

One of the things that always amazes me and that i like most is the fact that two or more can have the same book yet none of the pictures come out the same, even using the same media and colours you will get a very different picture, this is where the piece becomes your own work of art although DICEBIRD created the original line art and it will always be his, when you add your colours and your touch, much like Vandy Anderman did, it becomes your piece of art.

She did the colour on the back page and she did it beautifully. "Thank you Vandy for the beautiful piece and for allowing it's use".  By adding her own little swirls and lines as well as colour, she made this her own work of art !

If you will notice, along the outer edges of DICEBIRD's designs, there is a border. Try shading it in very lightly with coordinating colours or however you wish and see it take on a whole new form. It's lovely left alone but it is very lovely with a touch of colour as well.

DICEBIRD has an exceptional talent for creating beauty, combine that with his love of people and his love of sharing and this is what you get, art that comes from his heart and soul. I believe he would create even if there was no one there to see it ! This is his first of many books and I hope to be a part of all of them.

Hope you enjoy,

Athena McNeill
Supporter and friend of DICEBIRD

This Book is made in partnership with Athena Dawn Mcneill
This Book is dedicated to Athena Dawn Mcneill, DICEBIRD's Mom
and www.beepackaging.com

Many thanks to all the facebook coloring community for their support

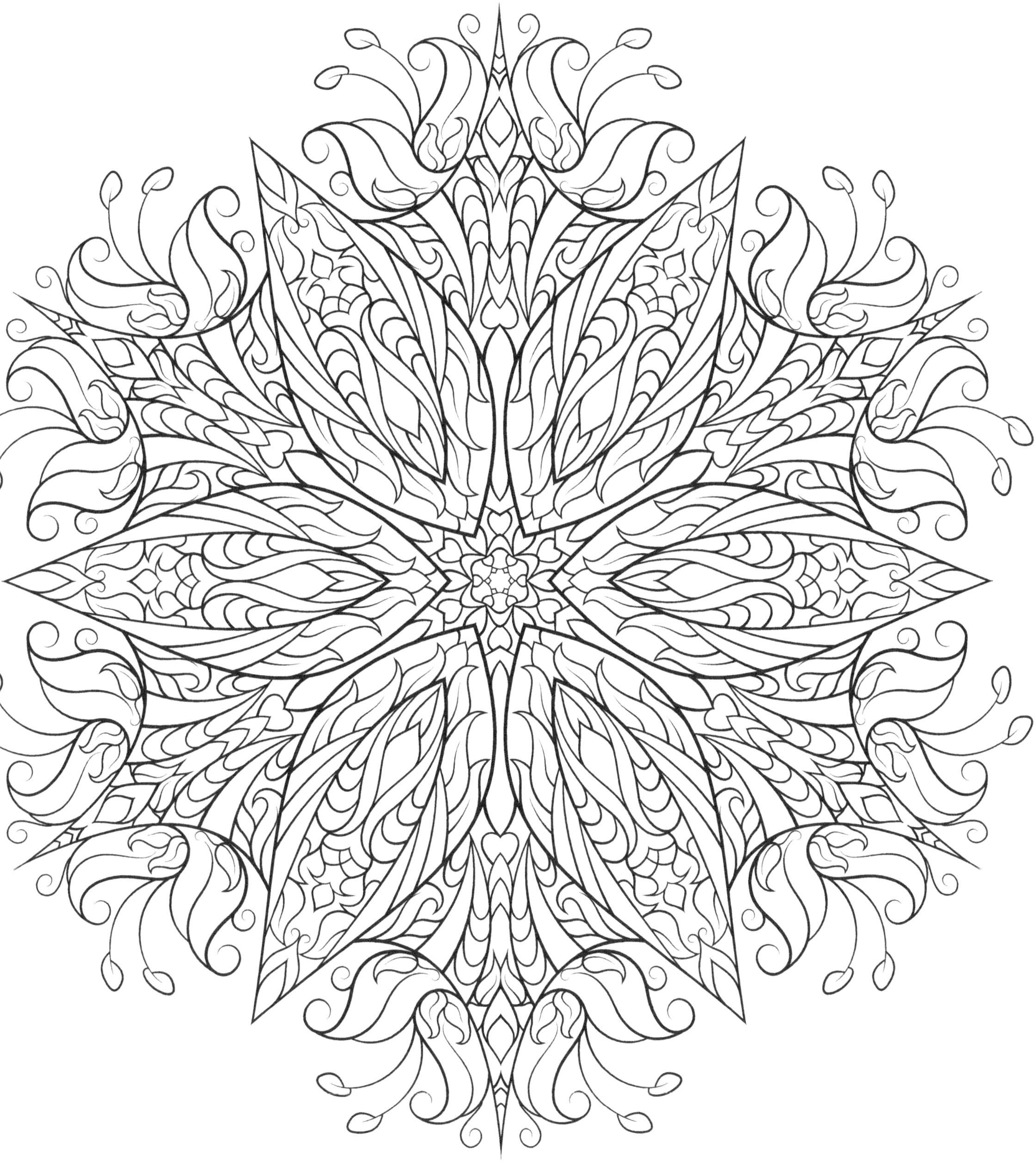

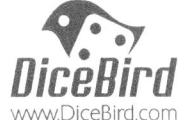

Freedom

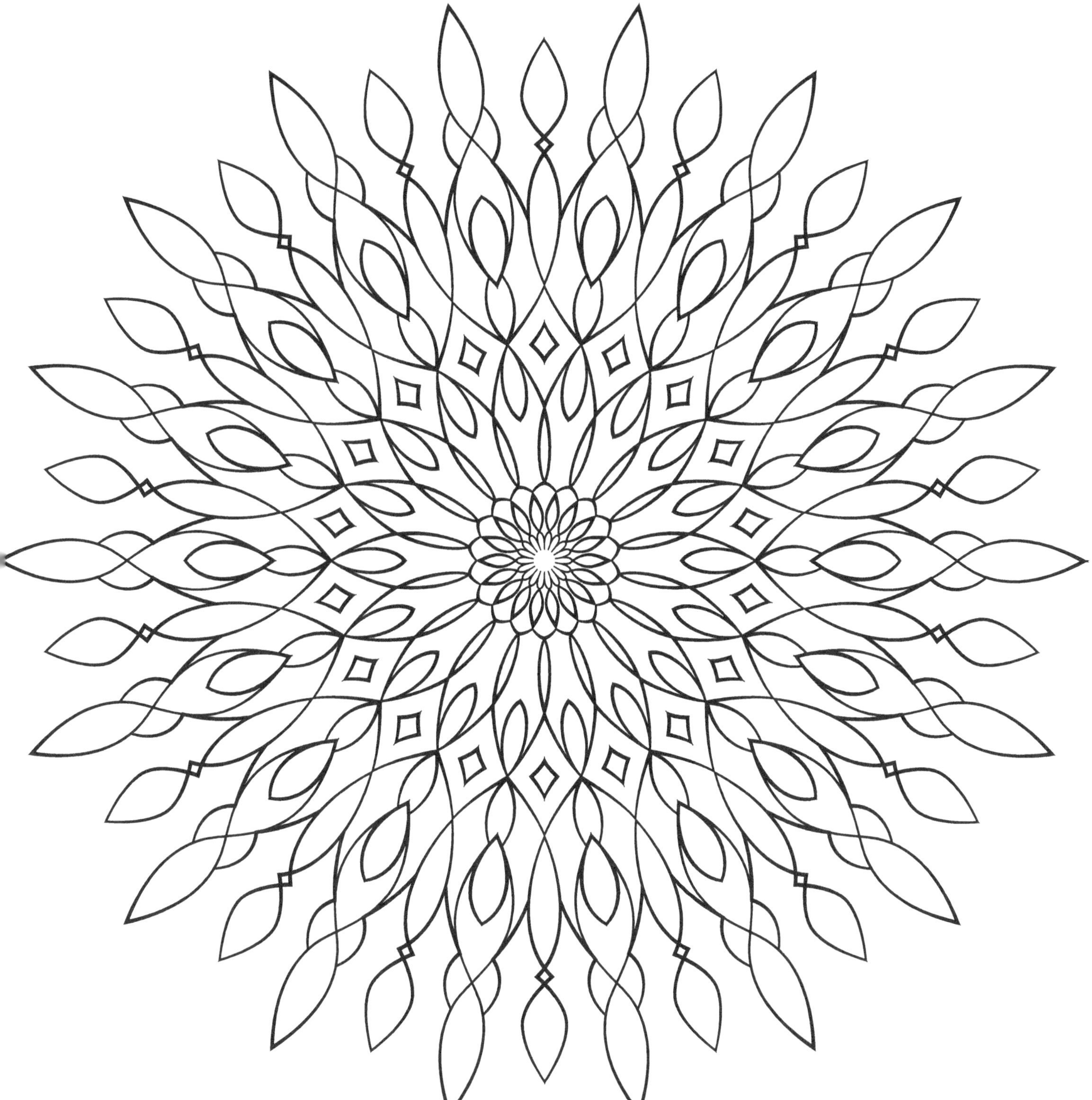

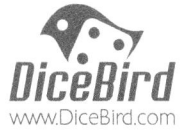

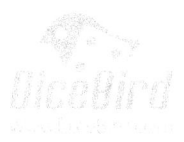

Luster

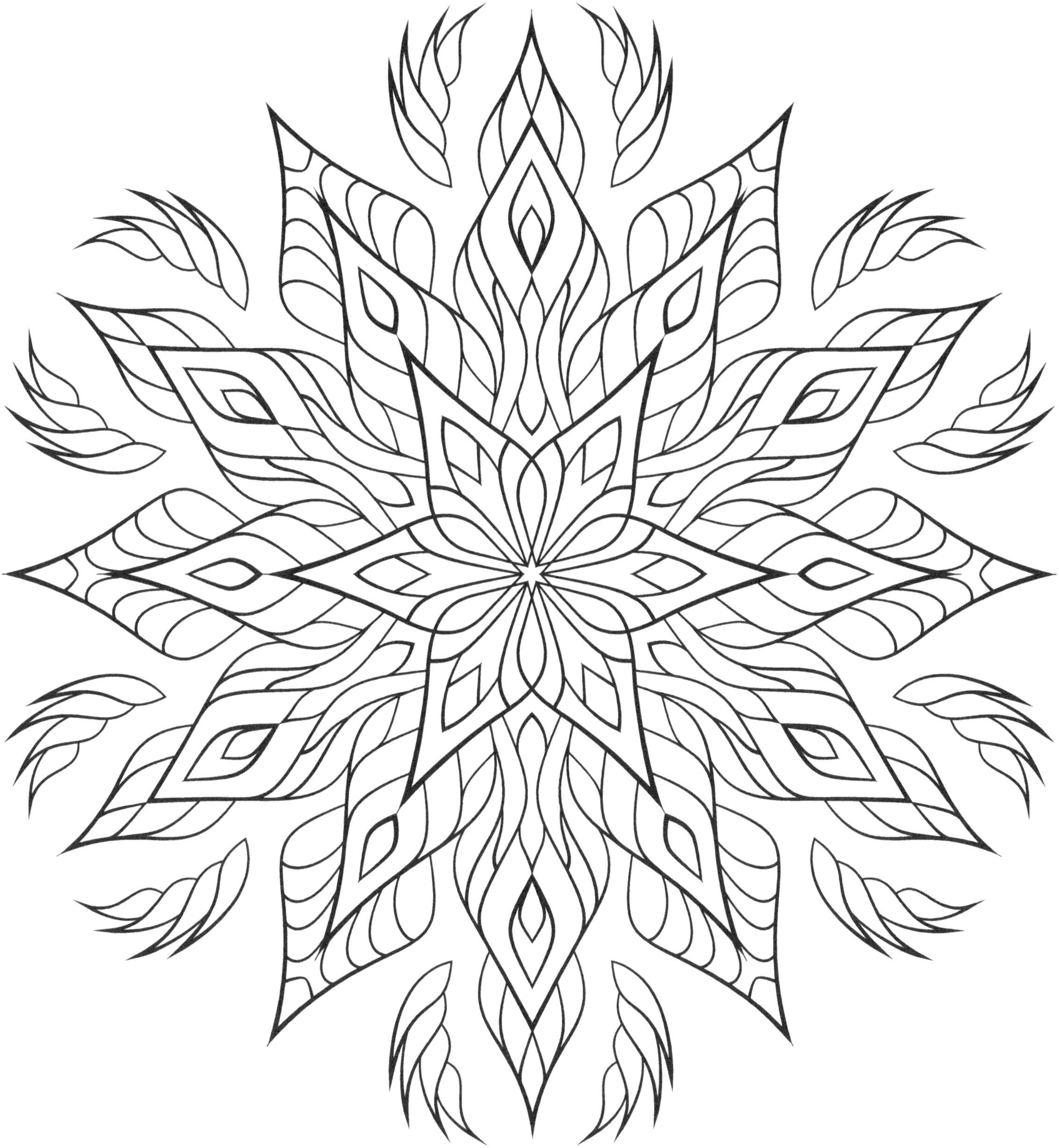

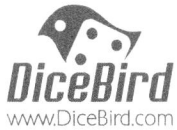

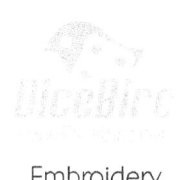

Embroidery

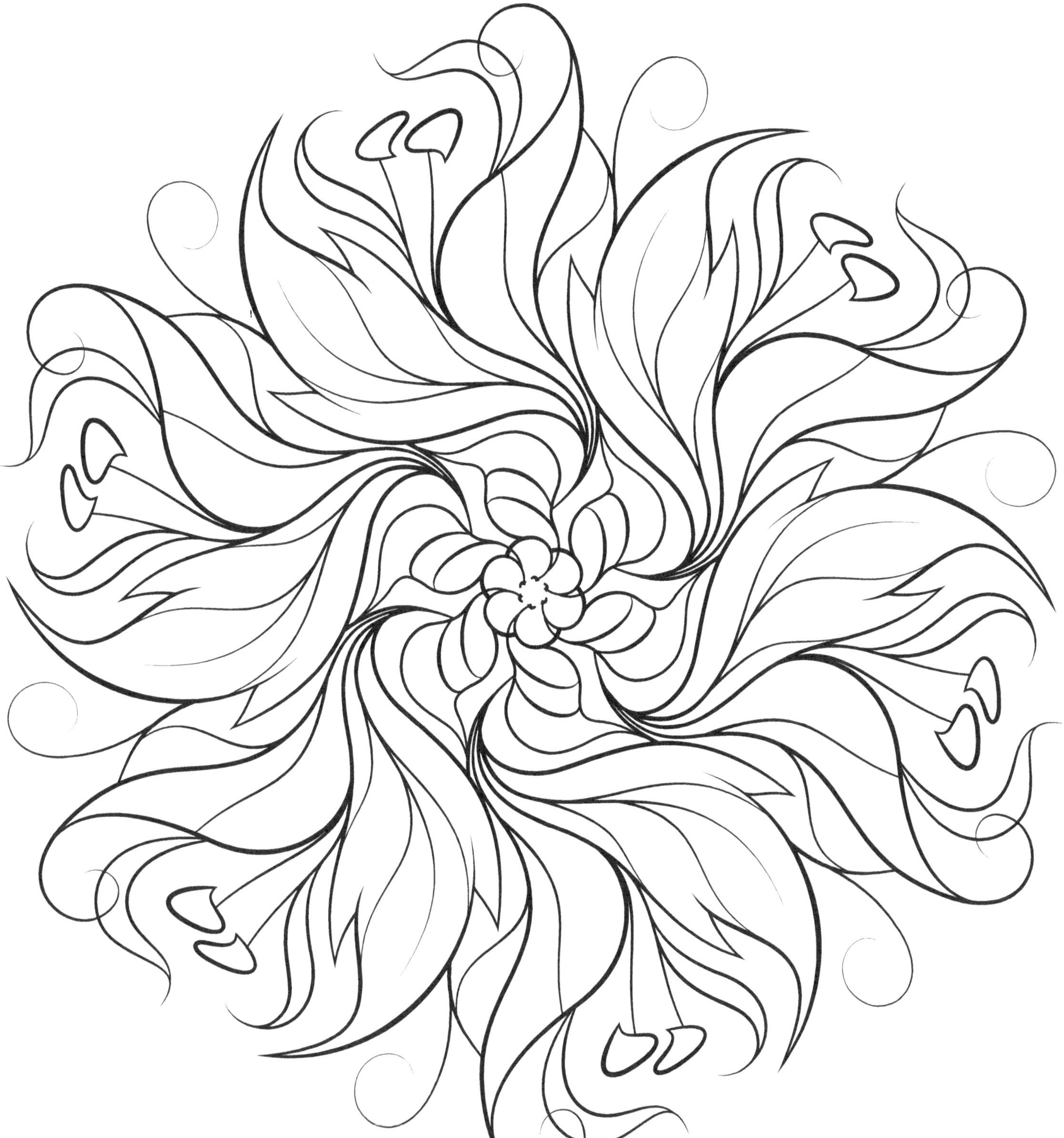

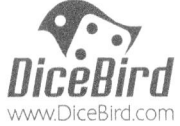

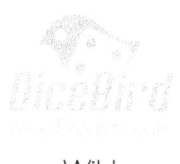

Wild

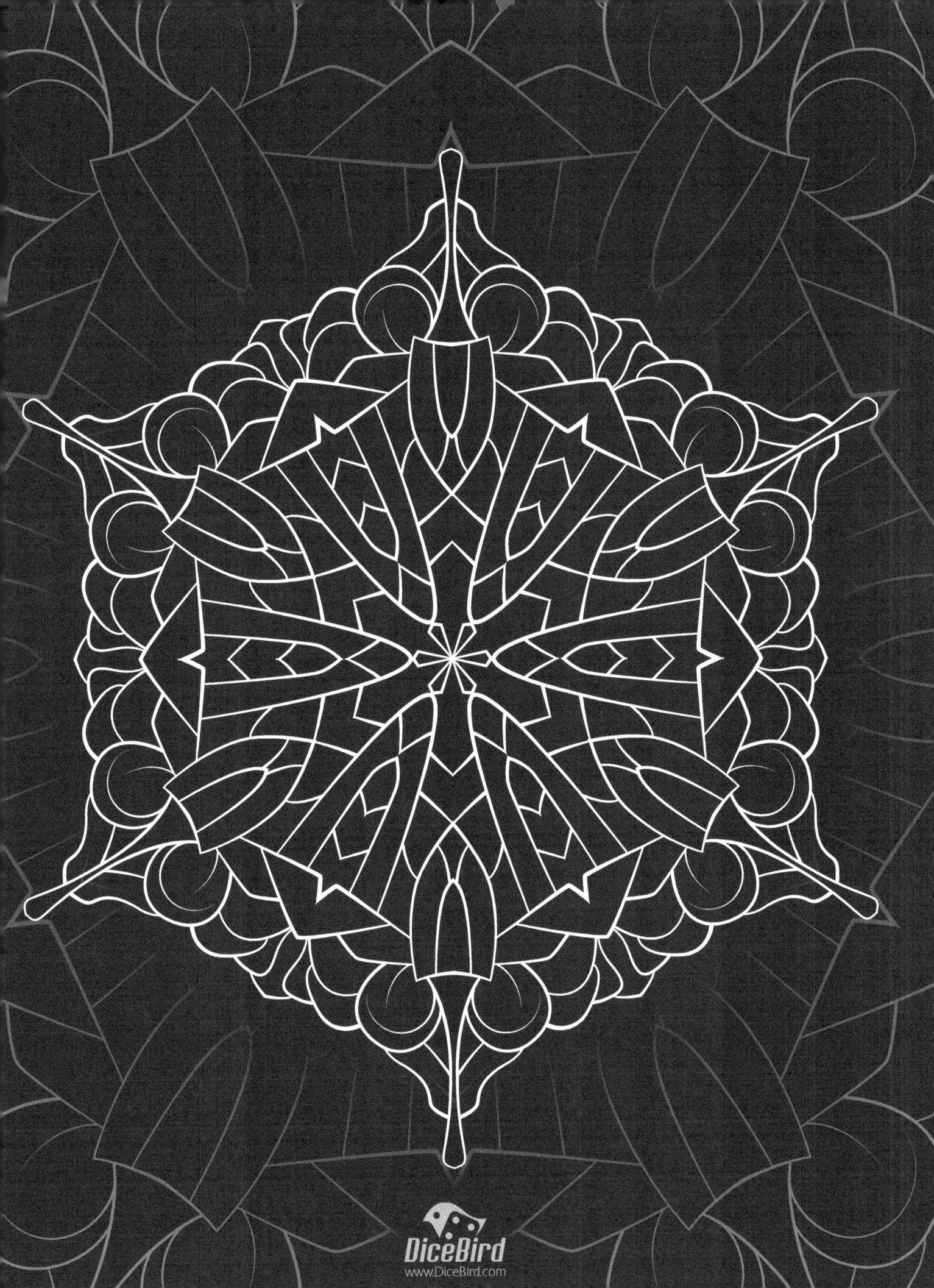

Star

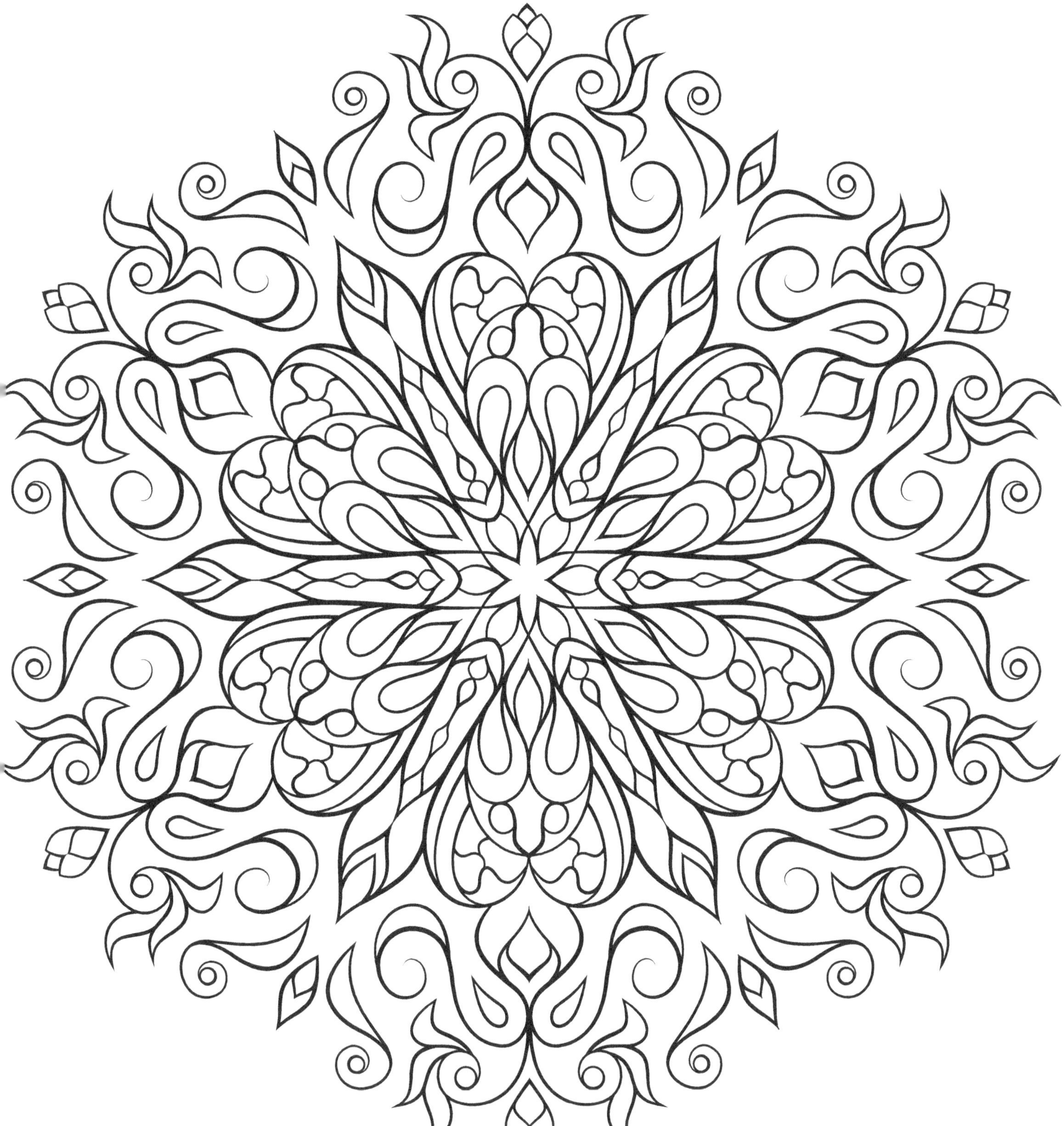

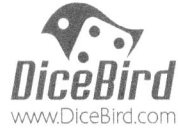

Open Heart

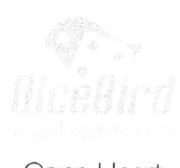

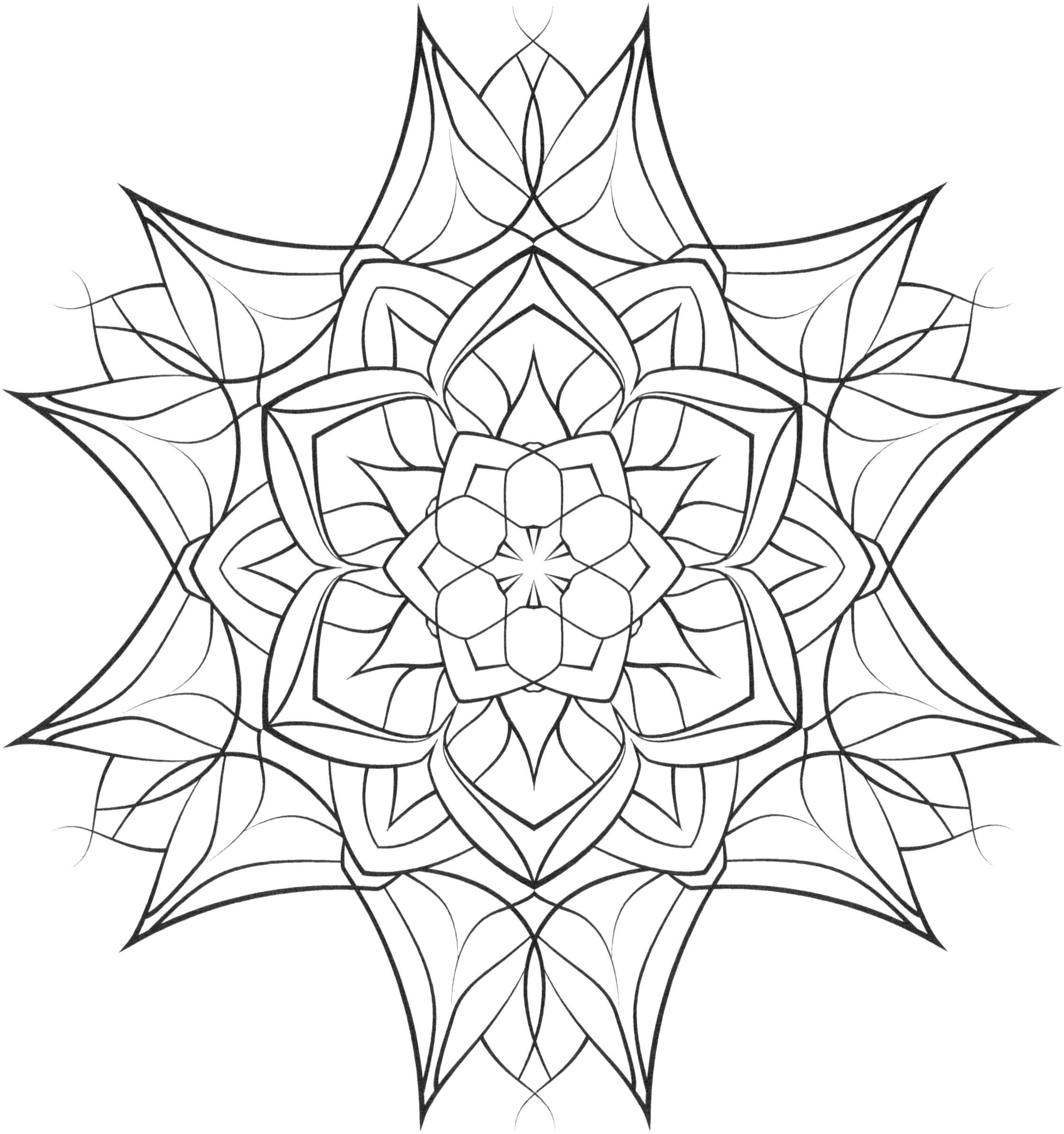

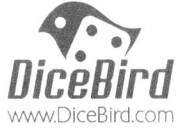

Perfume

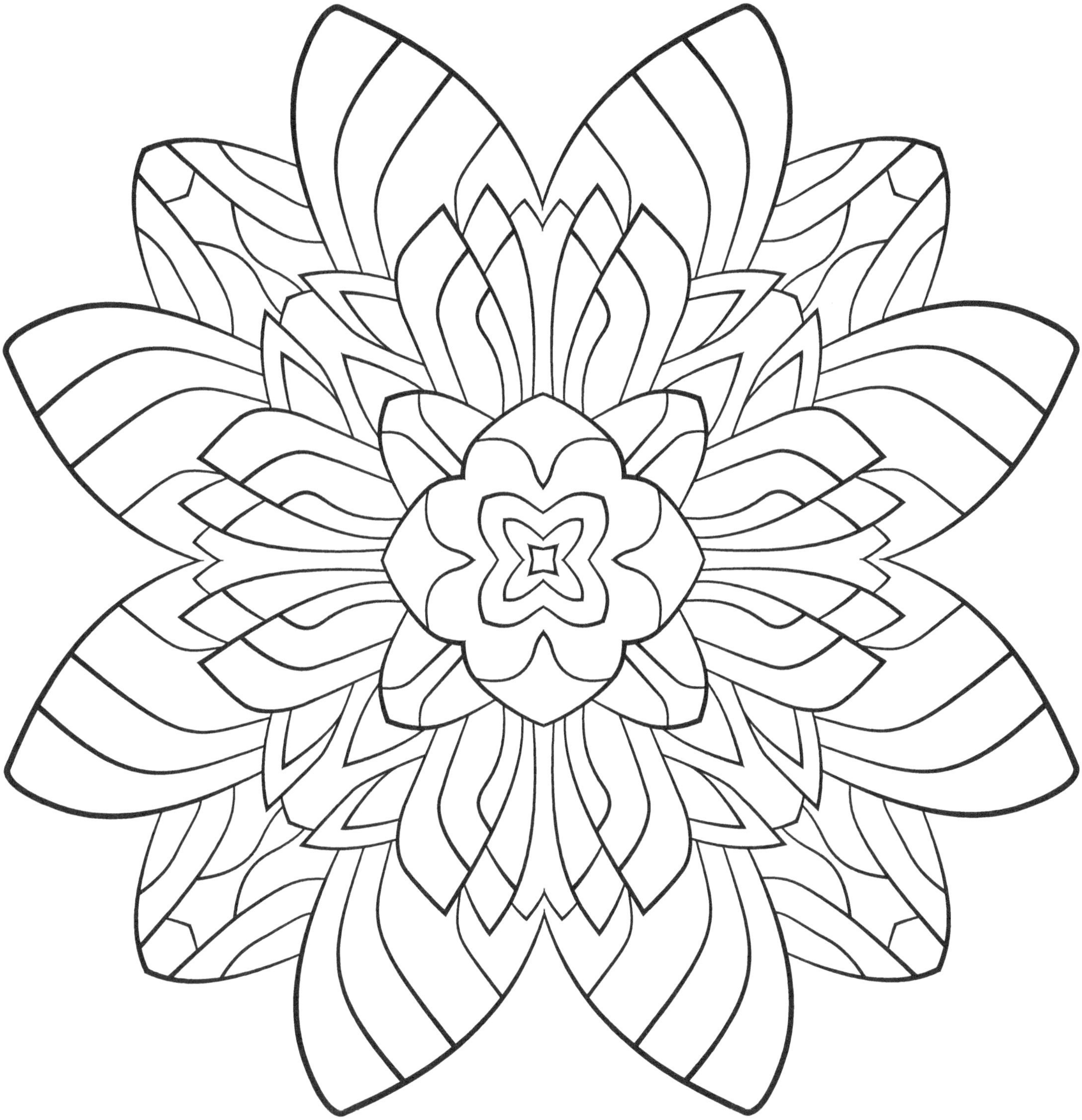

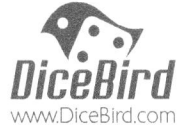

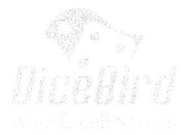

Eco

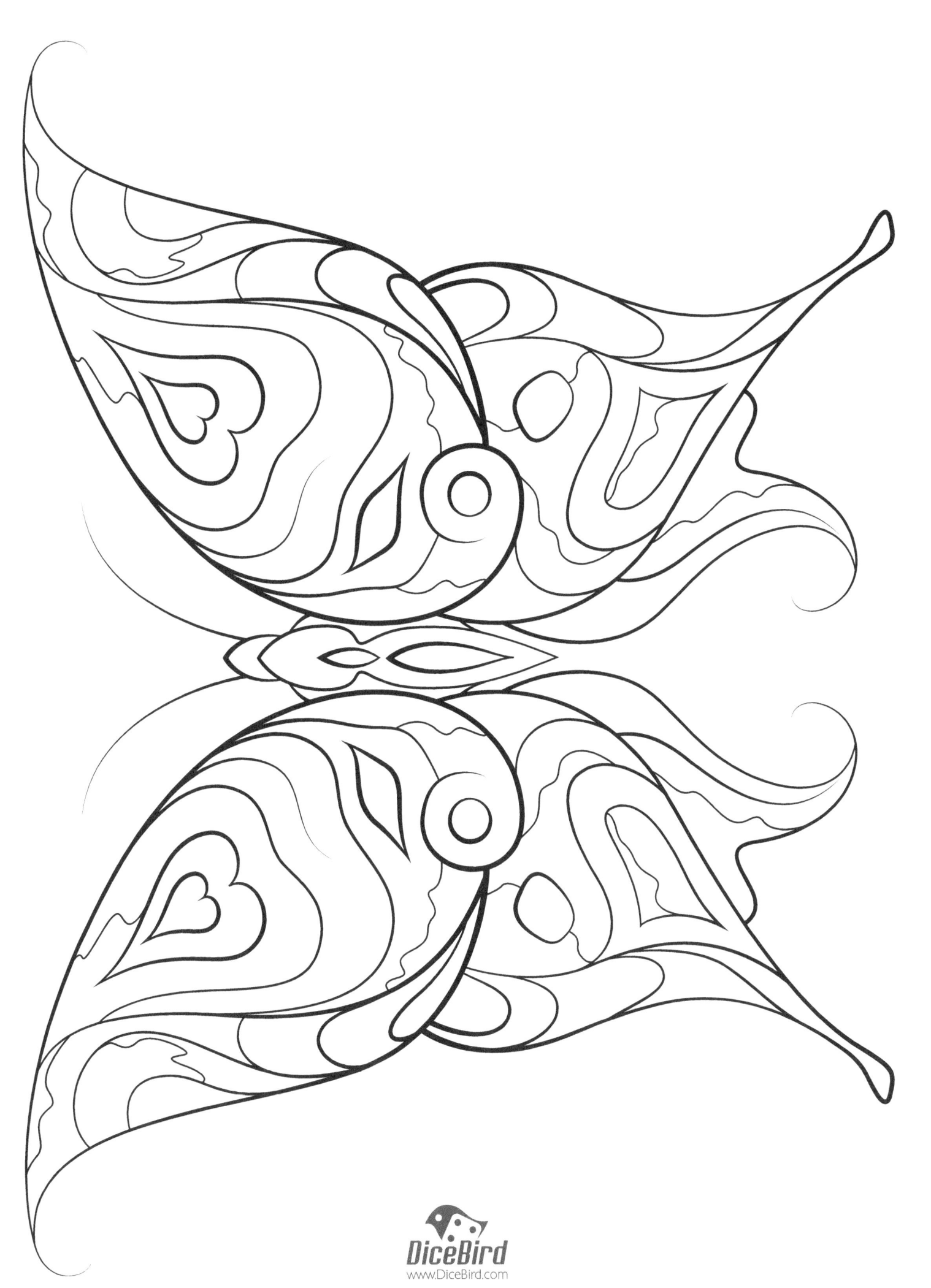

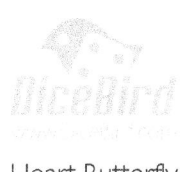

Heart Butterfly

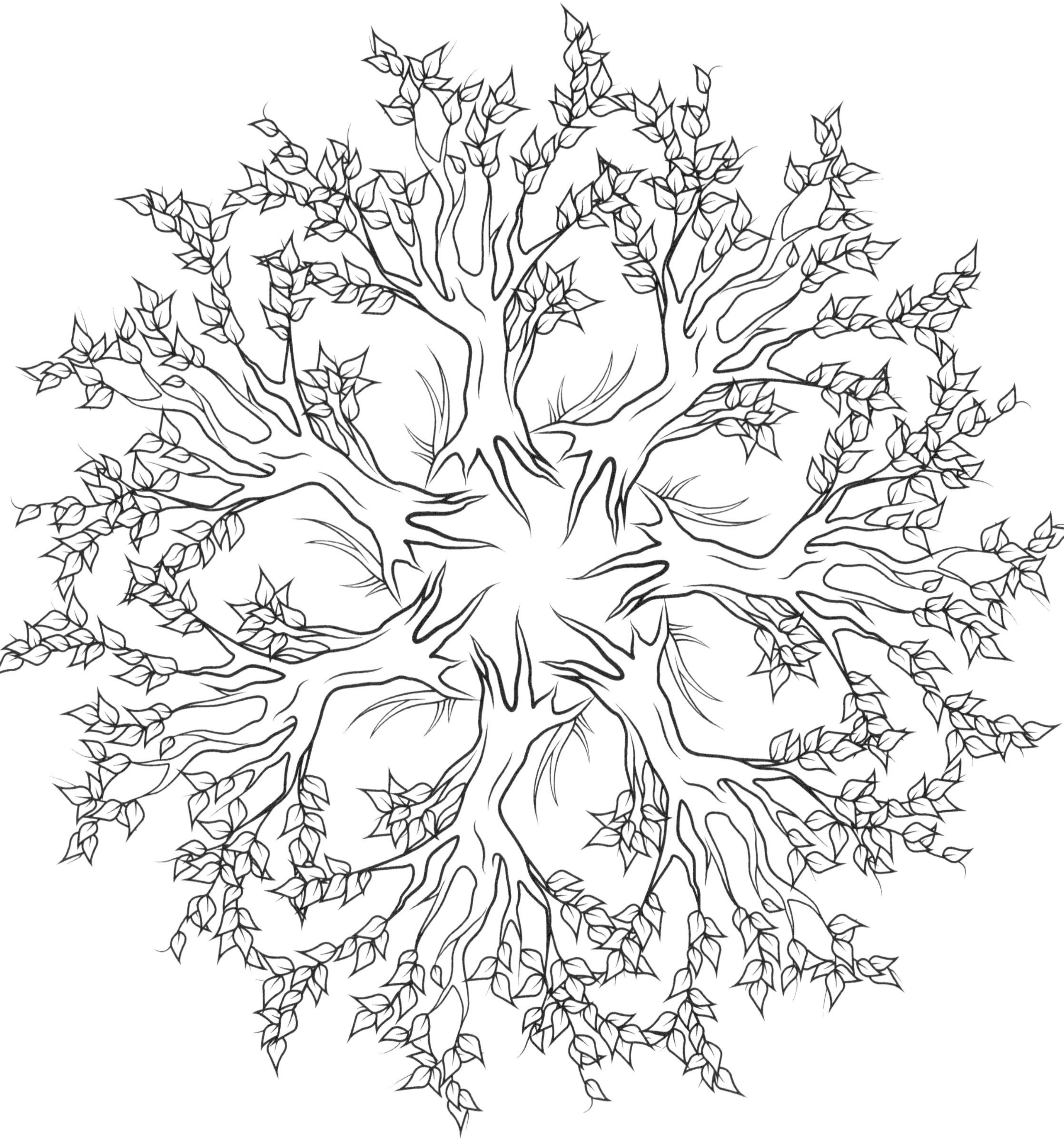

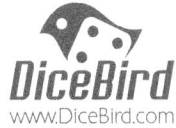

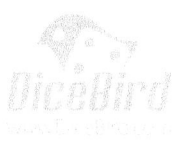

Tree

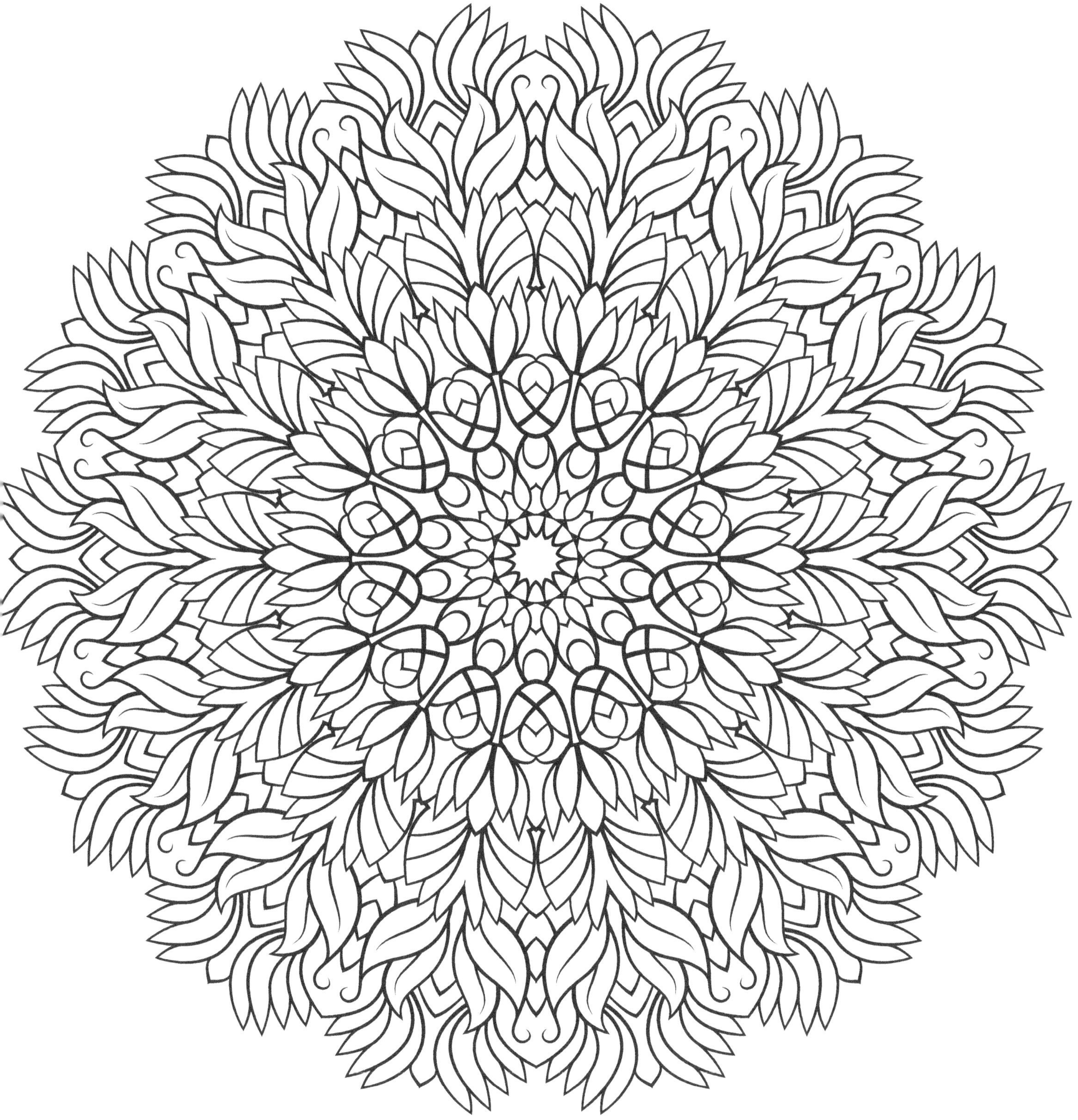

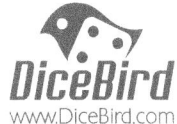

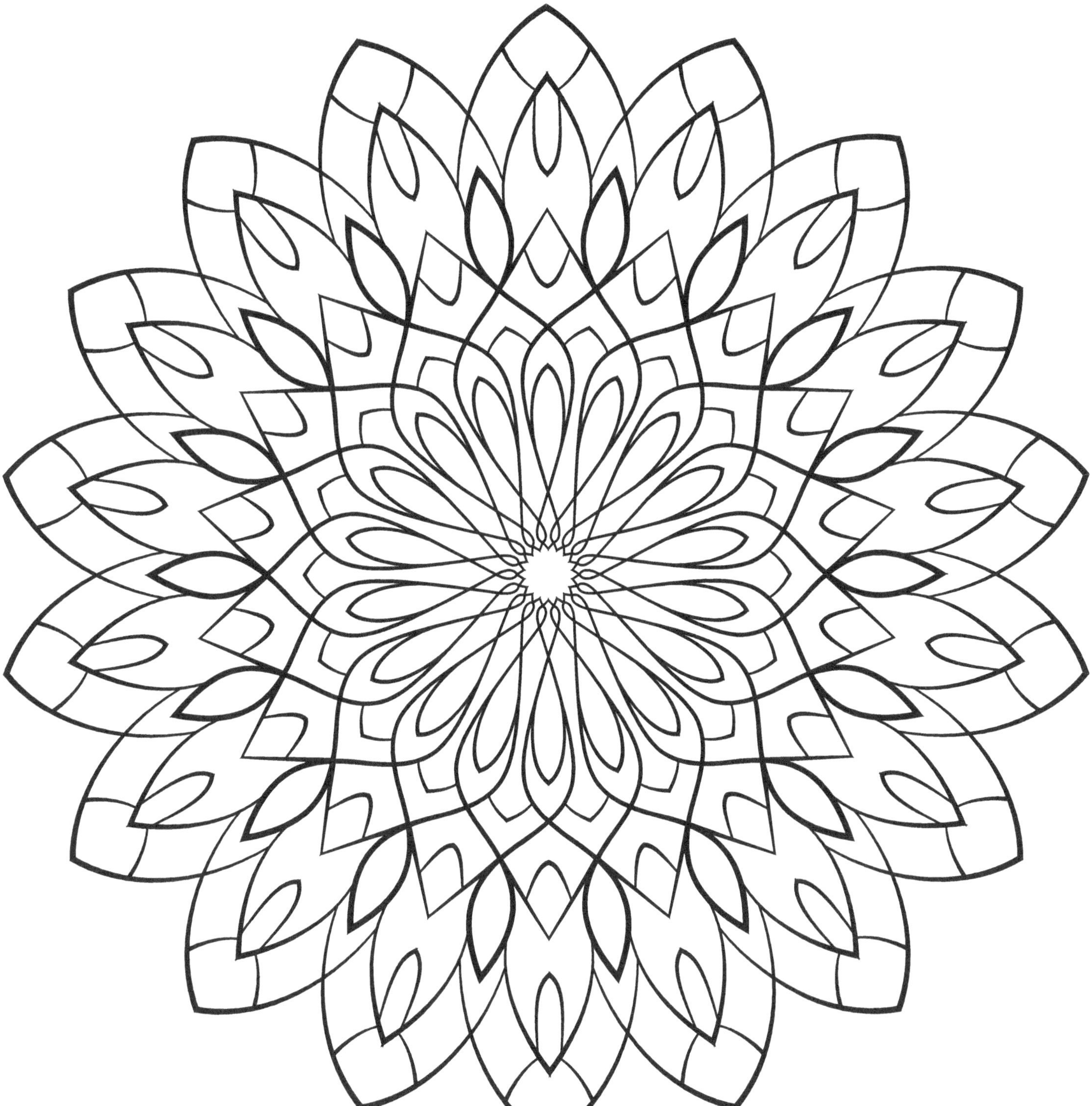

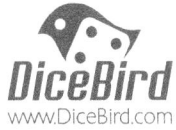

Venus

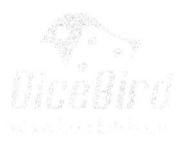

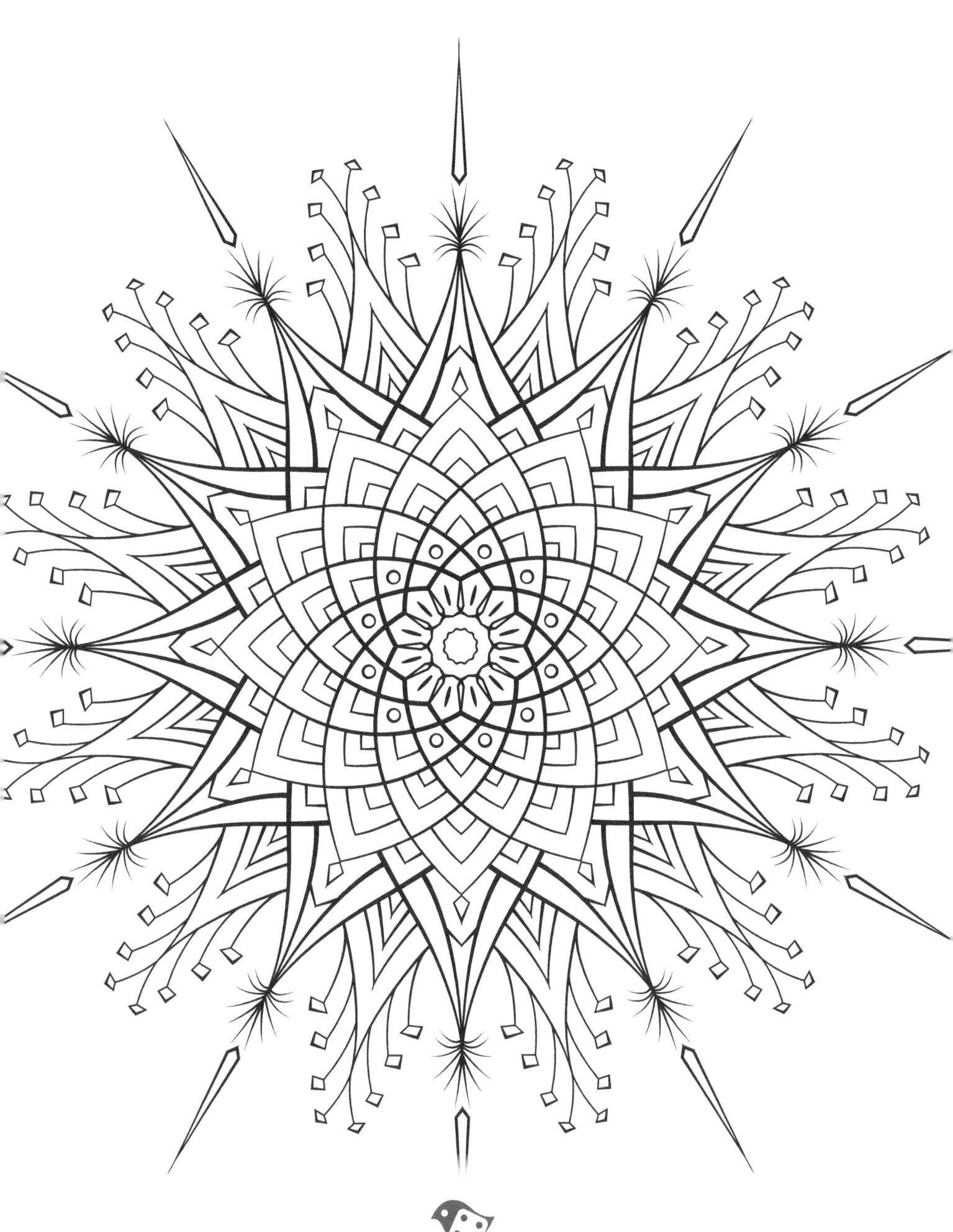

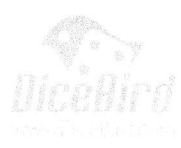

Party

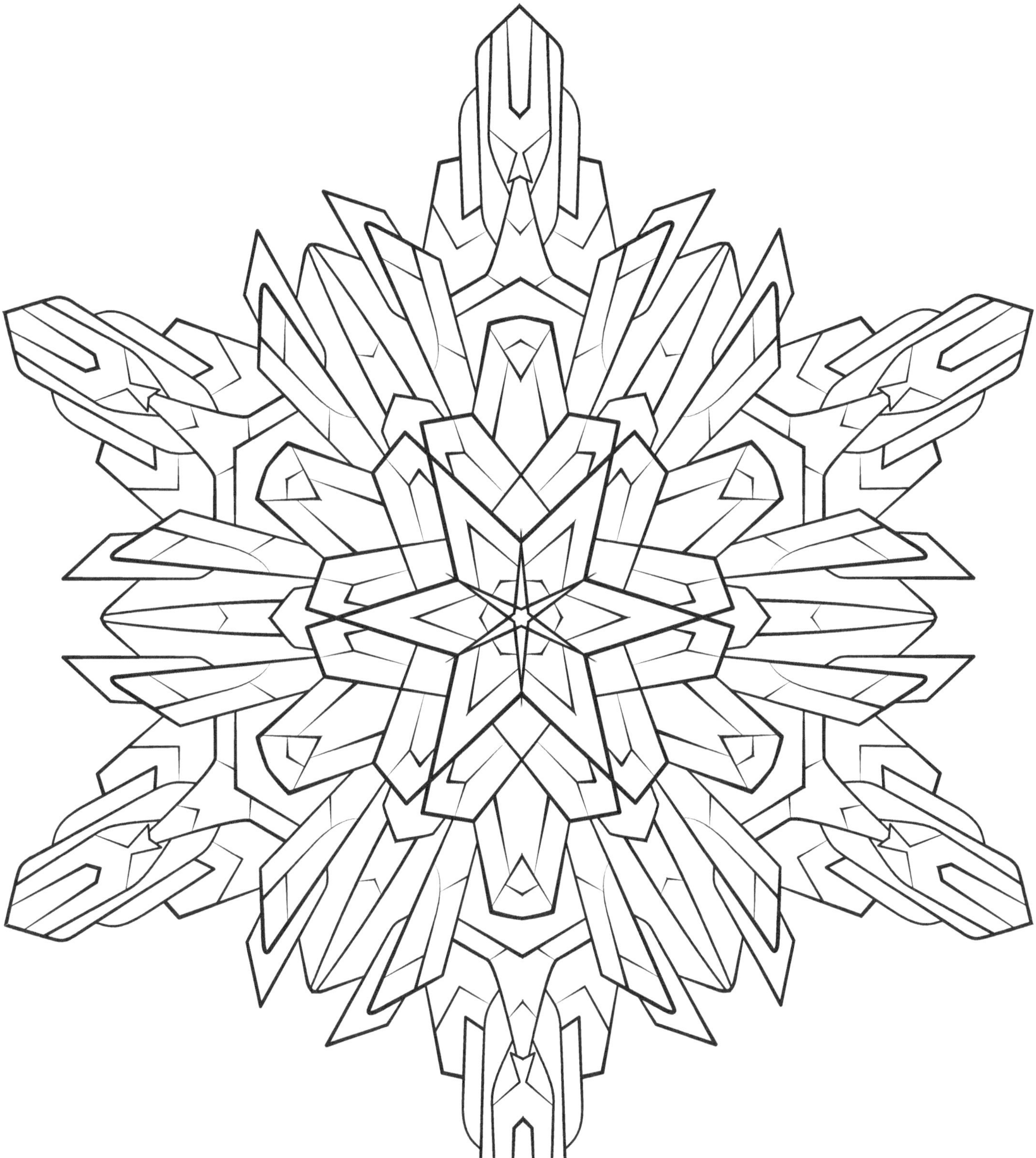

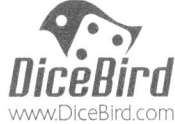

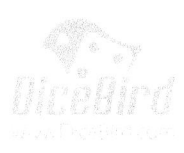

Quartz

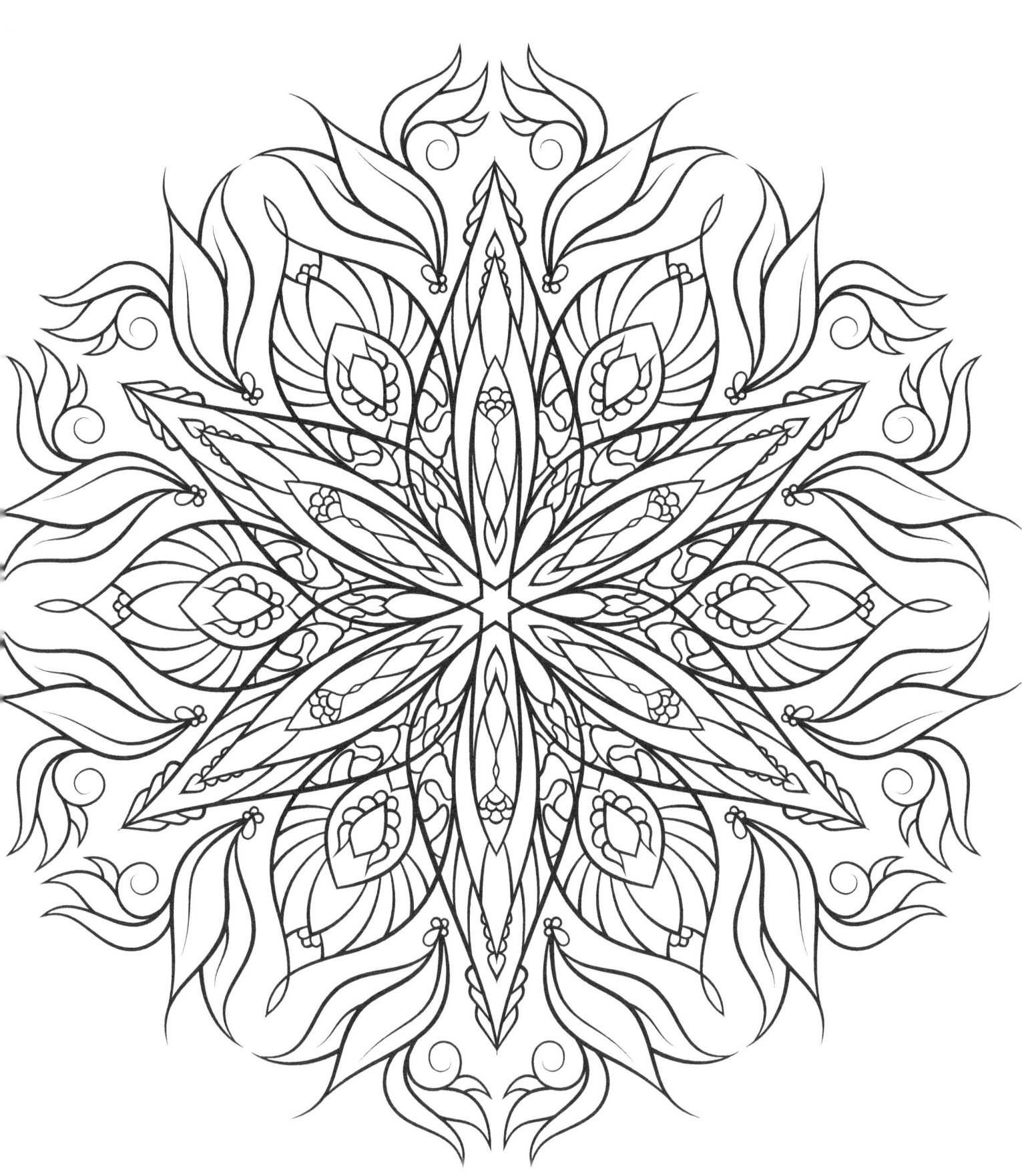

Crown

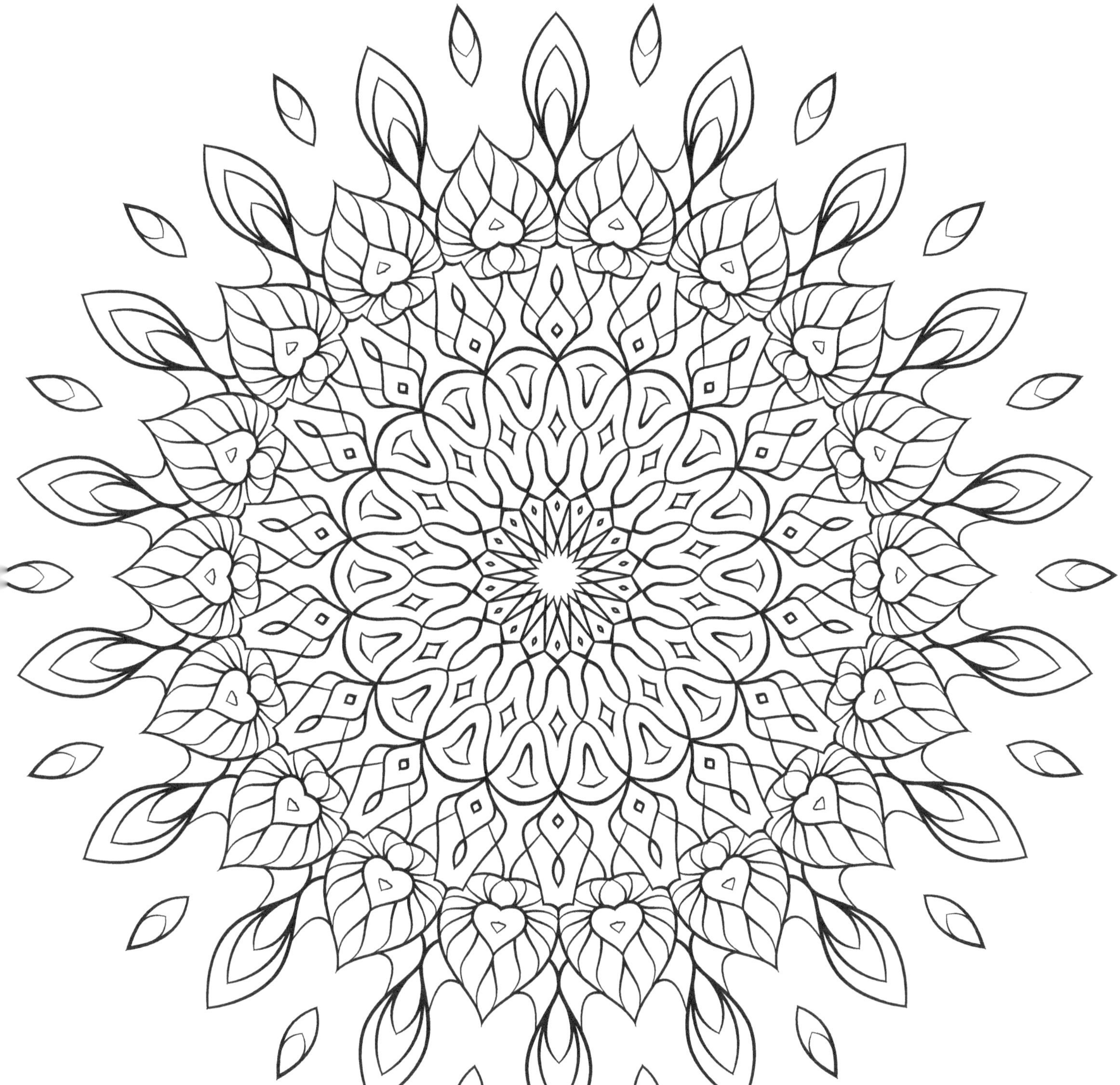

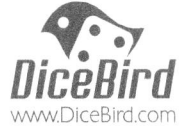

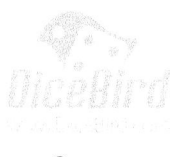

Queen

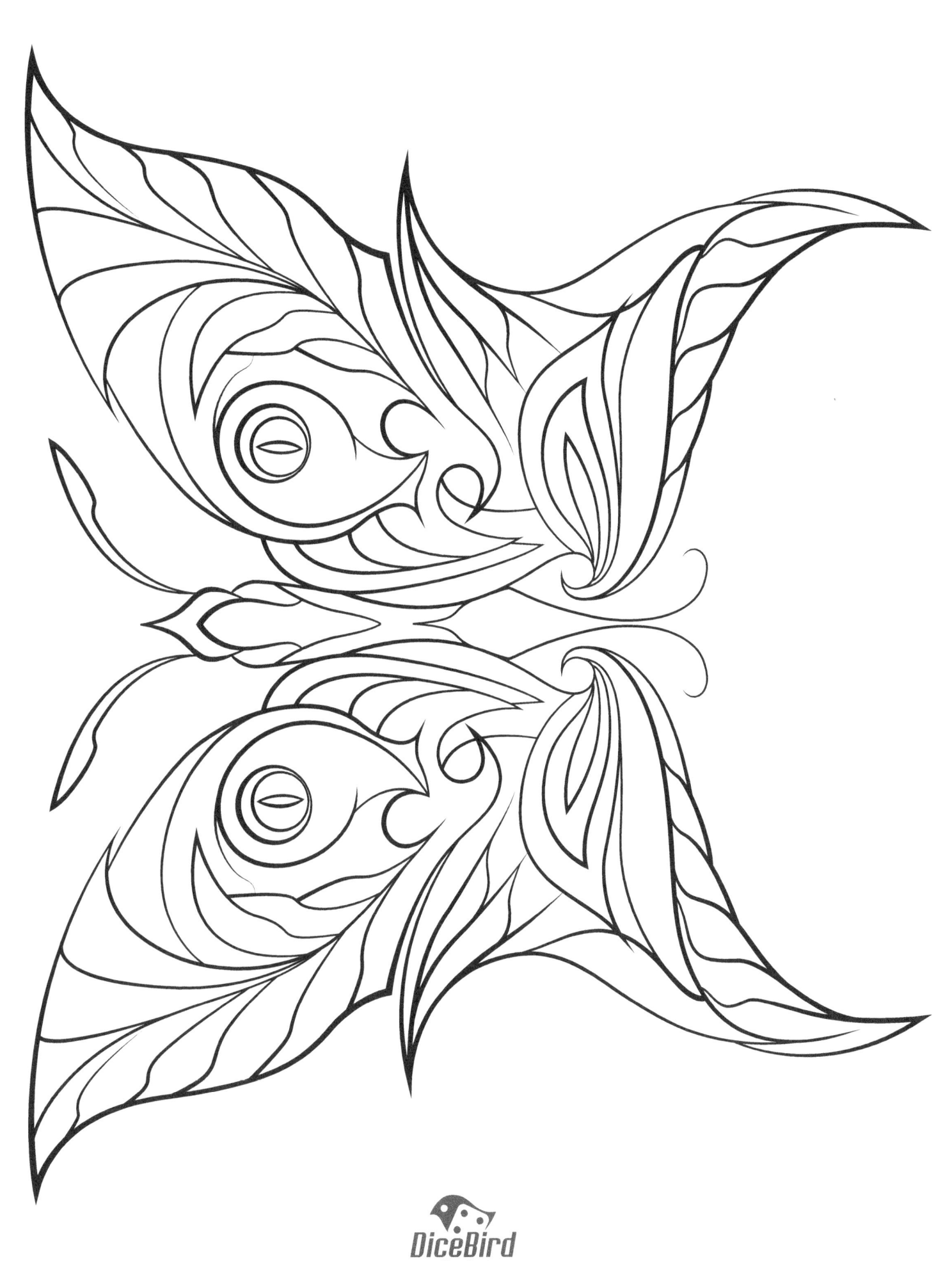

Butterface

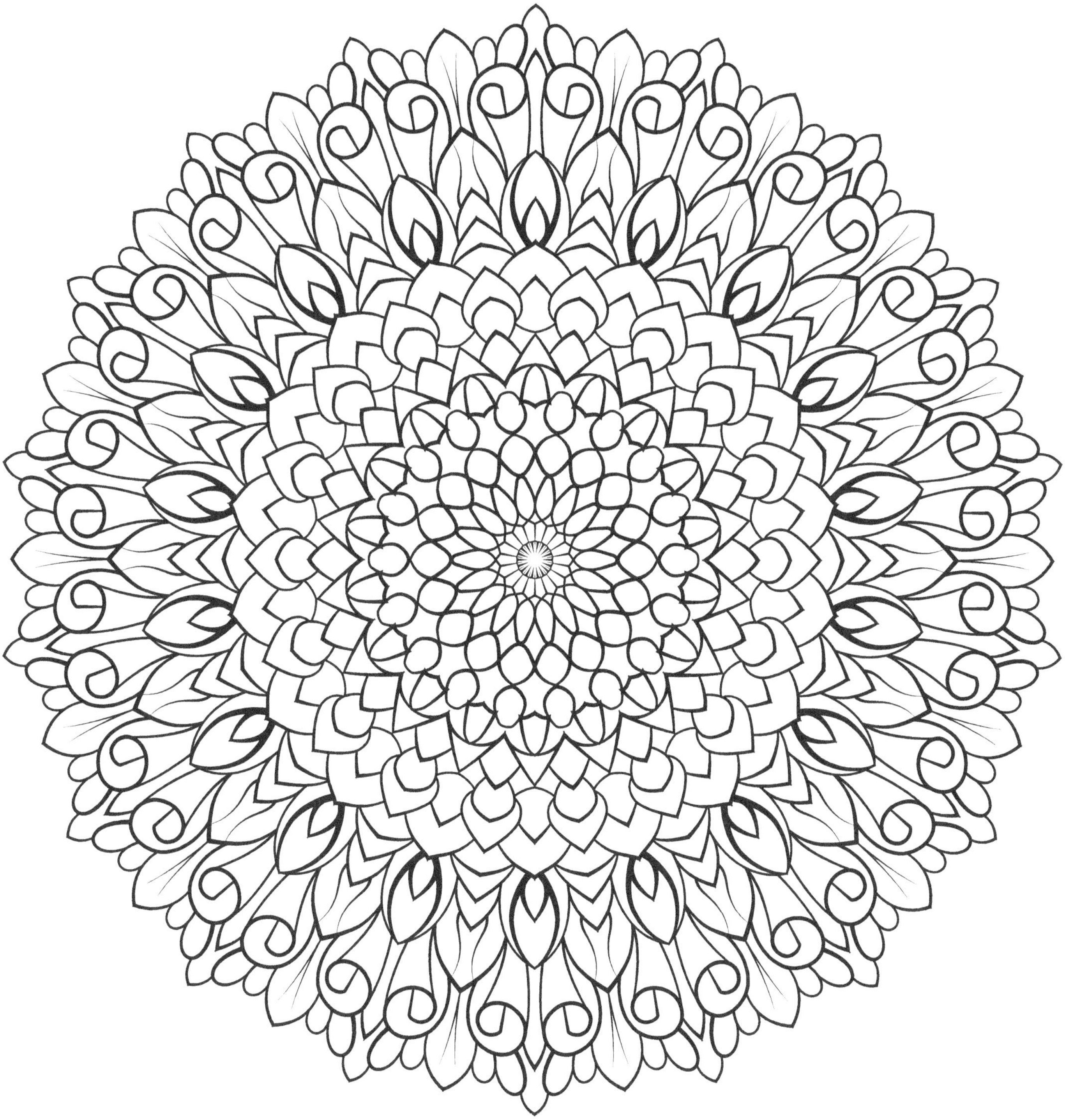

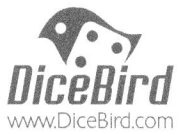

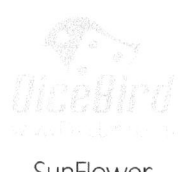

SunFlower

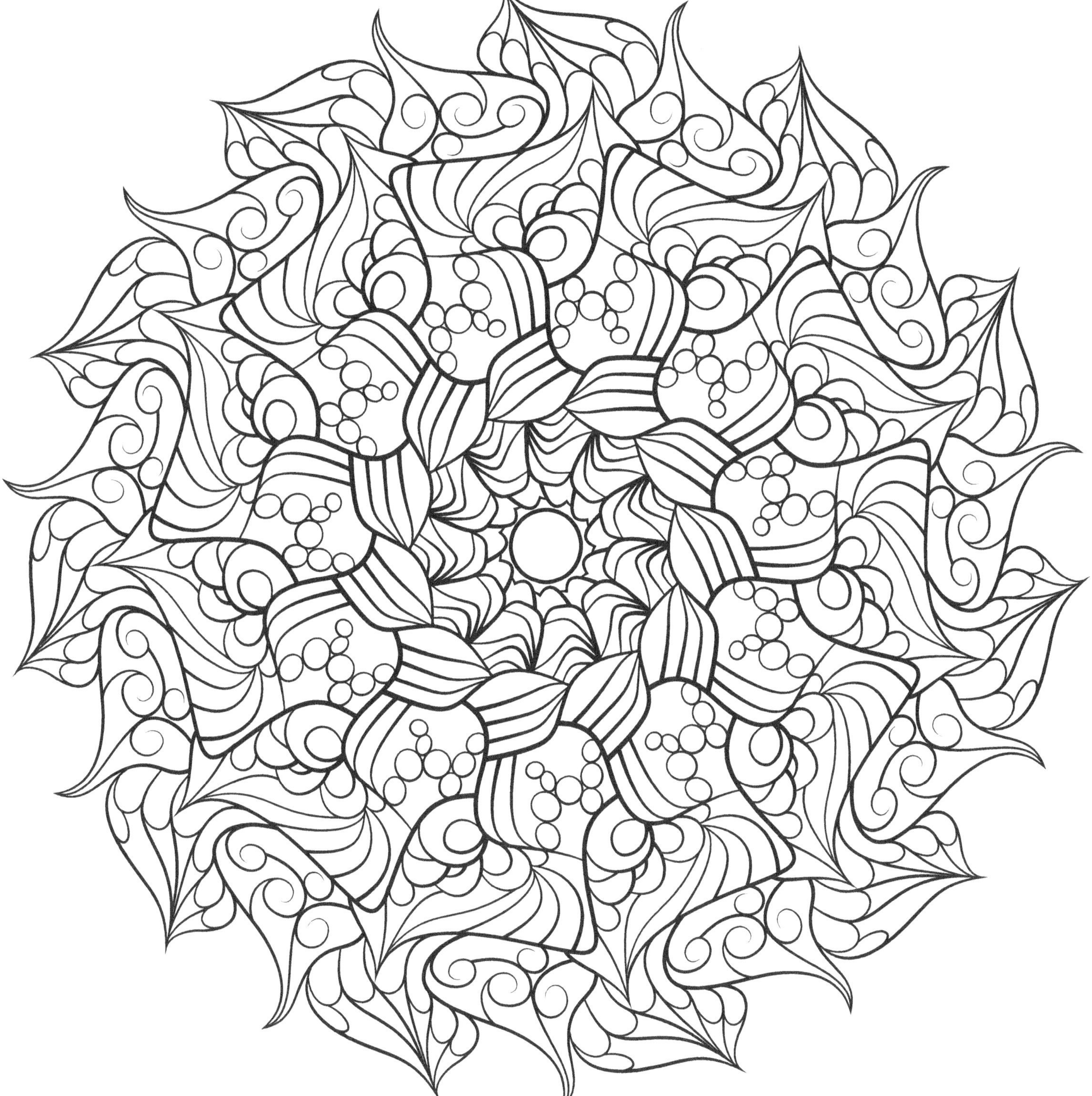

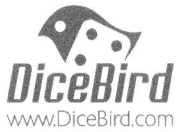

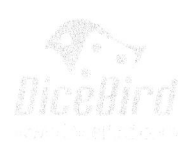

Merged

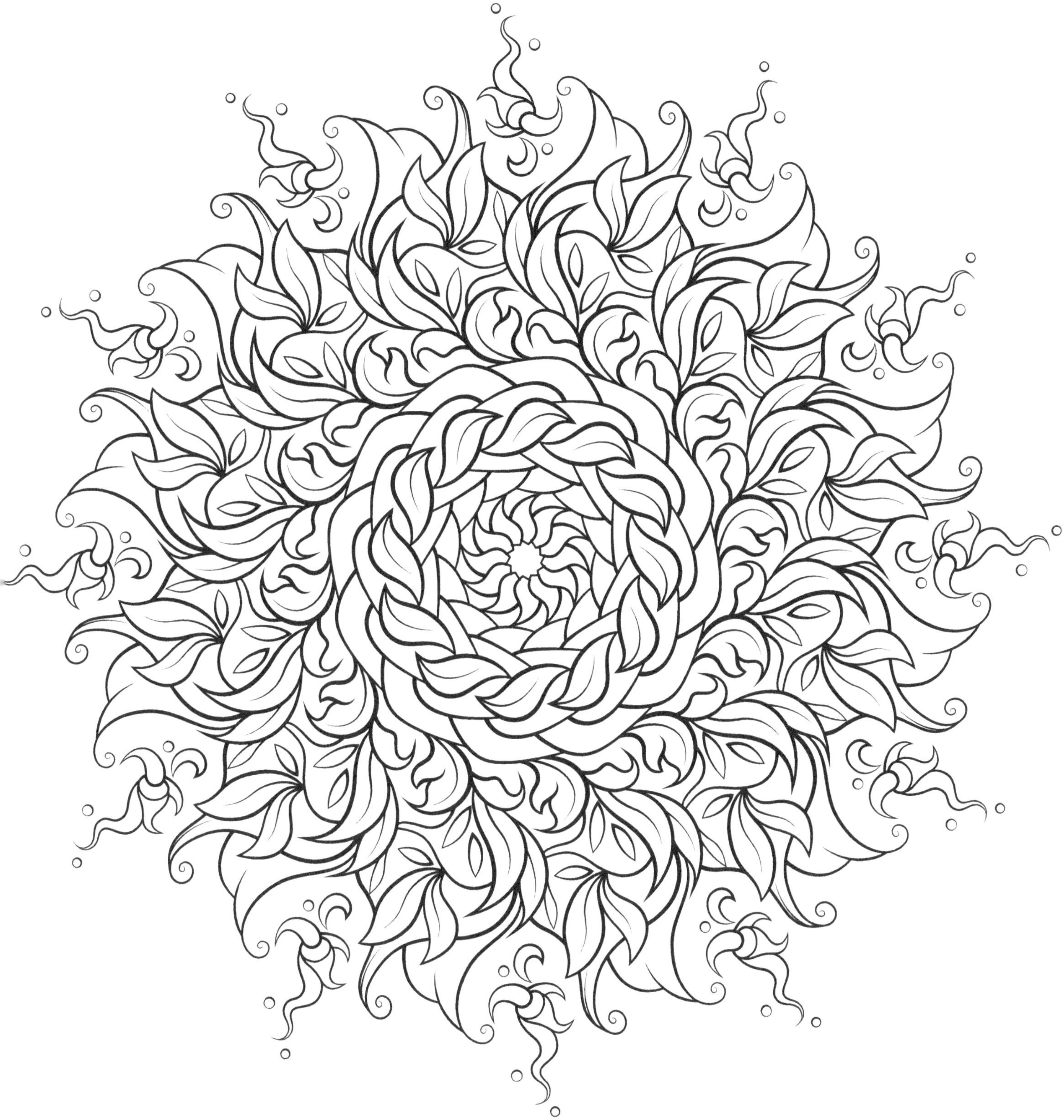

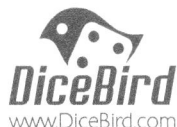

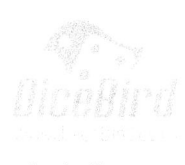

Little Forest

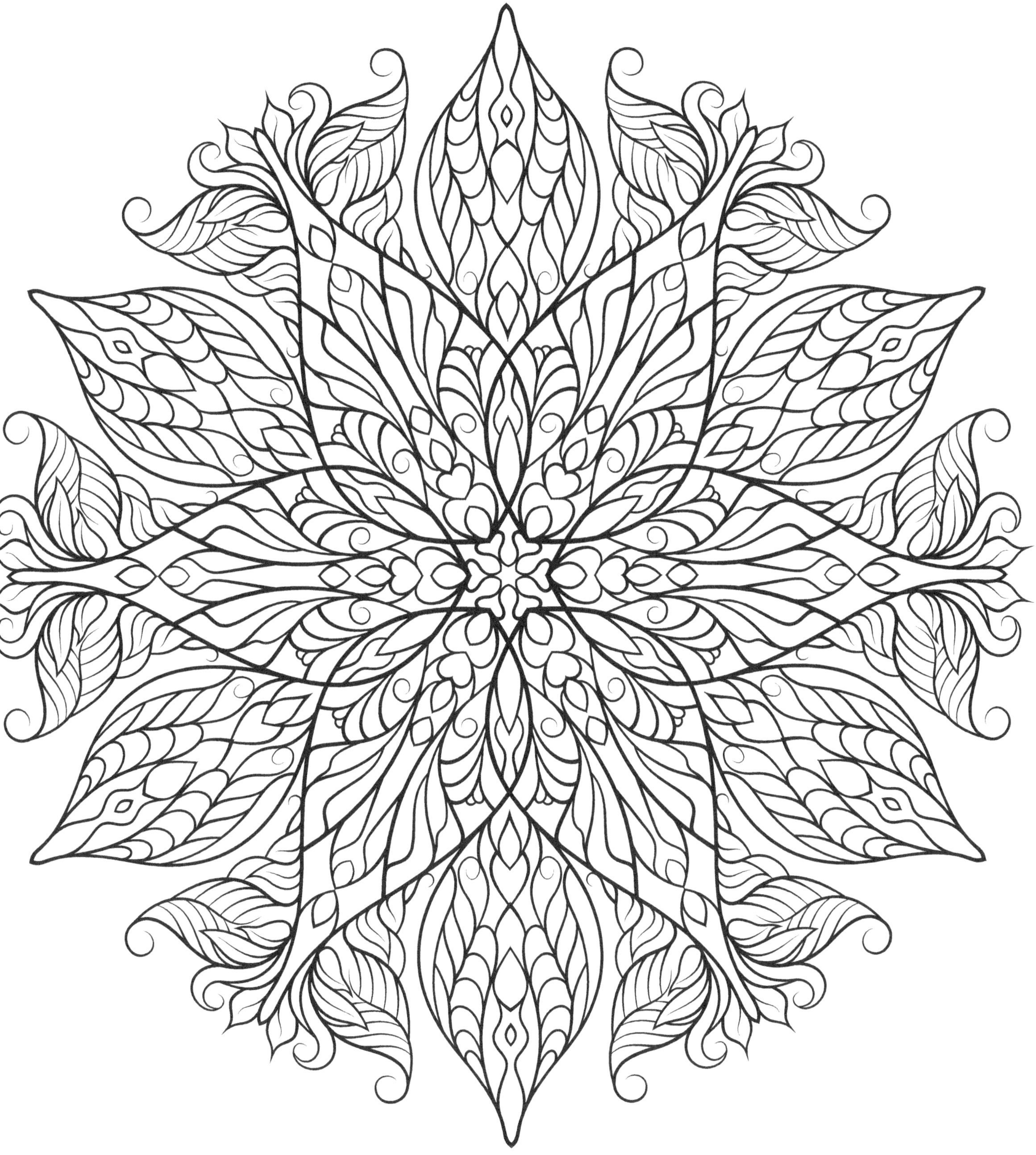

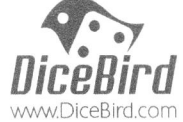

Mystery

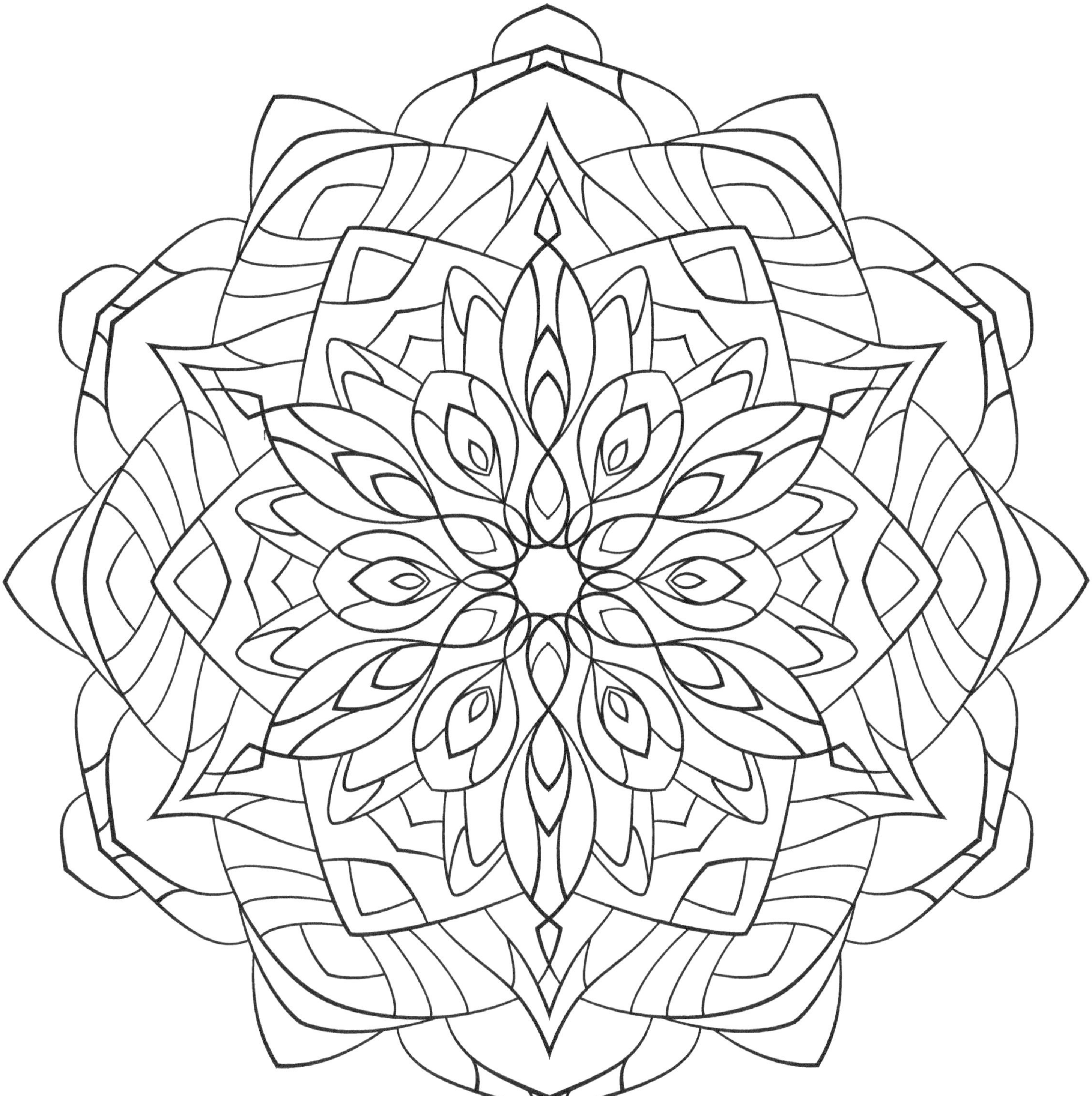

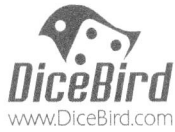

Elizabeth

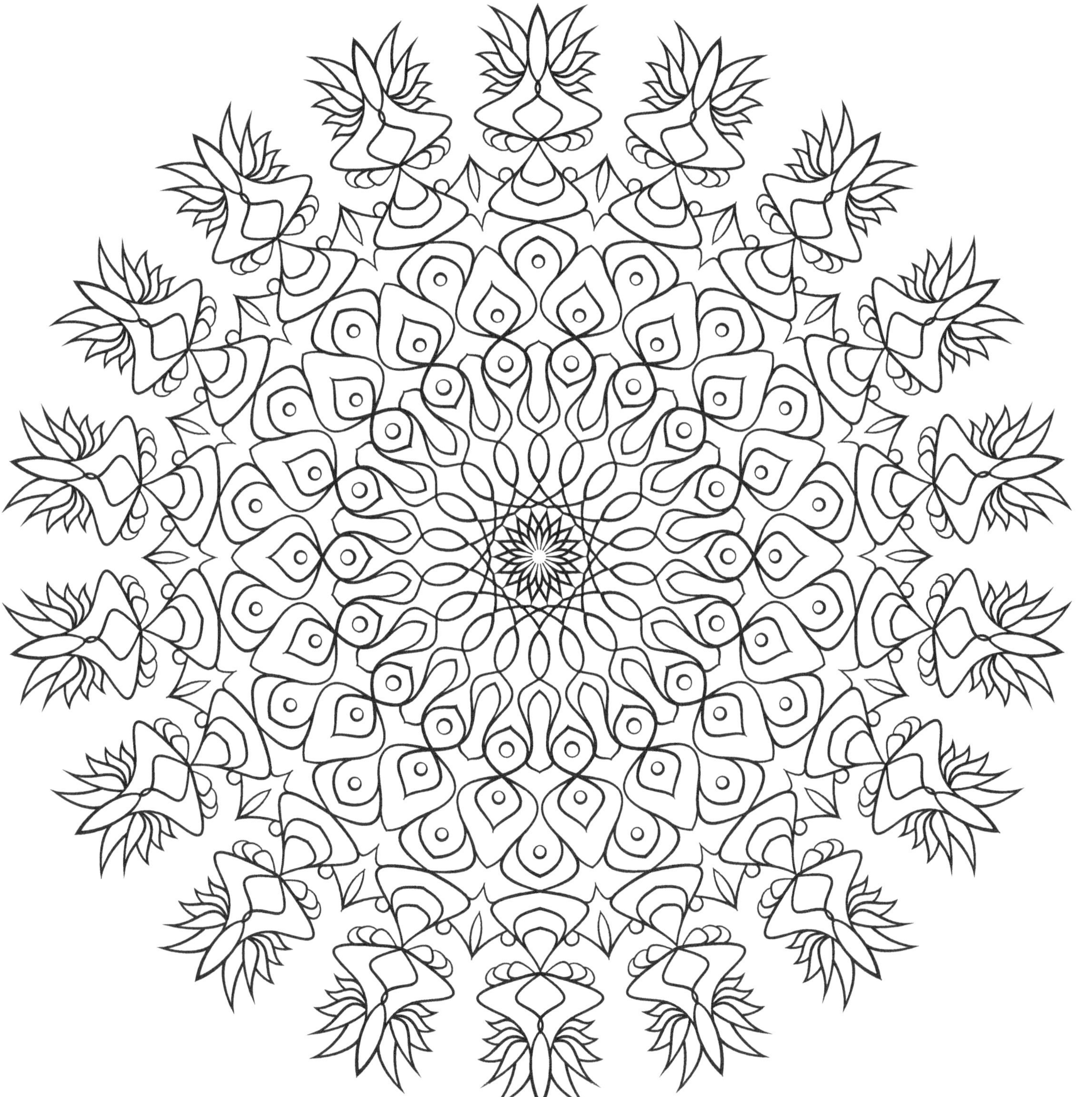

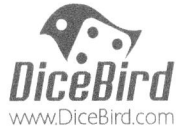

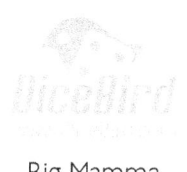

Big Mamma

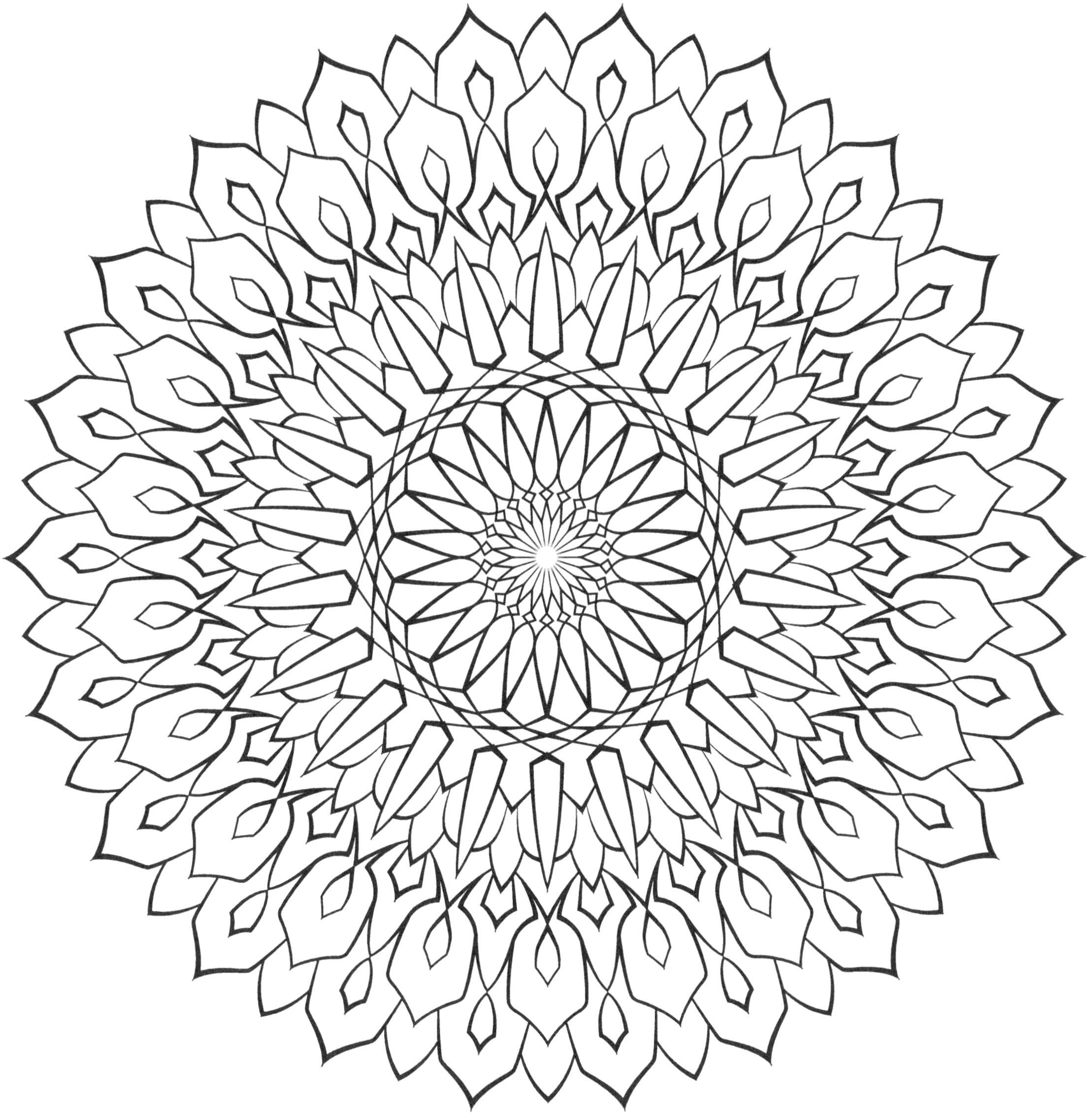

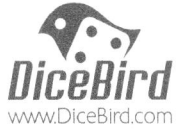

MoonFlower

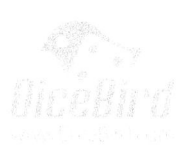

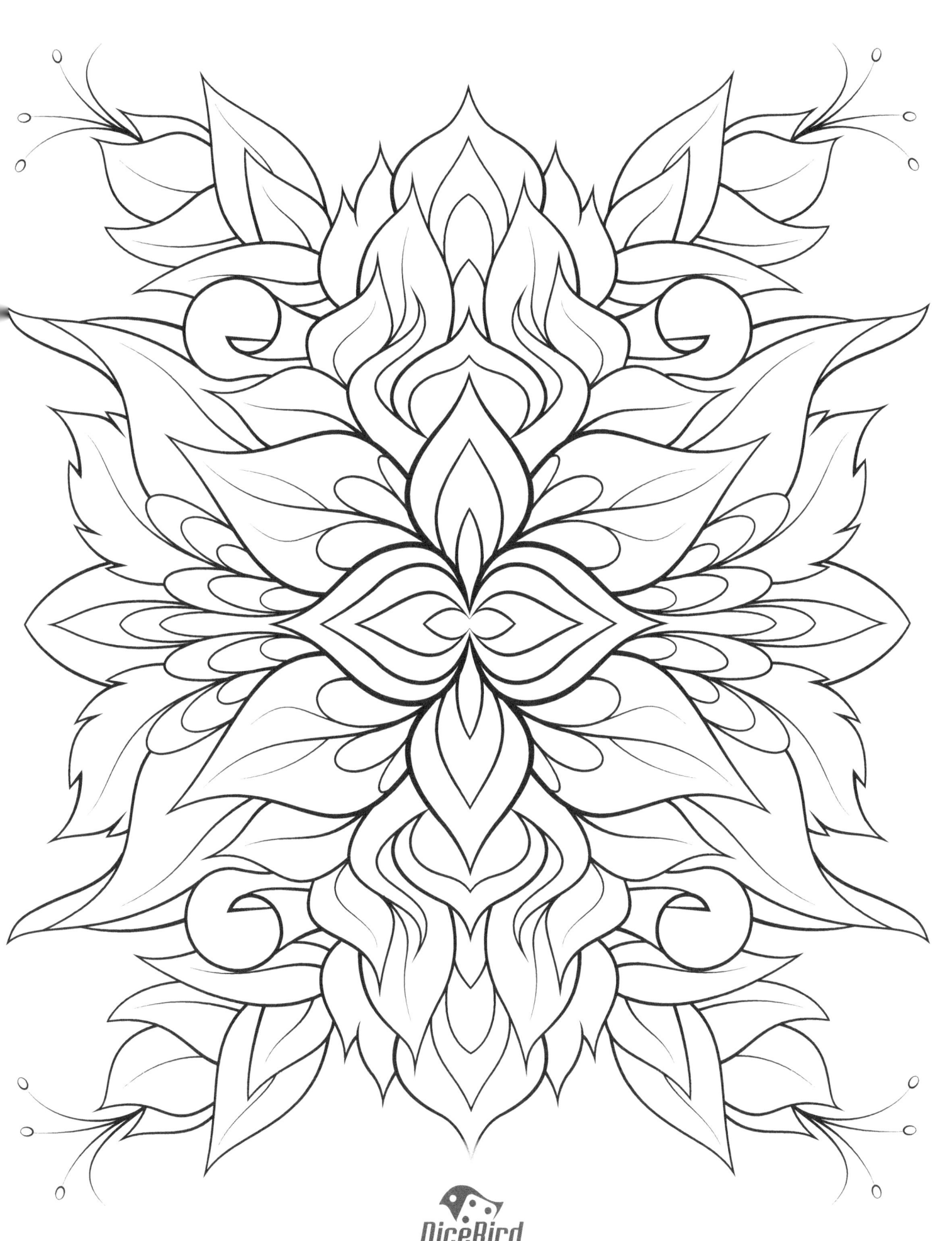

Mutation

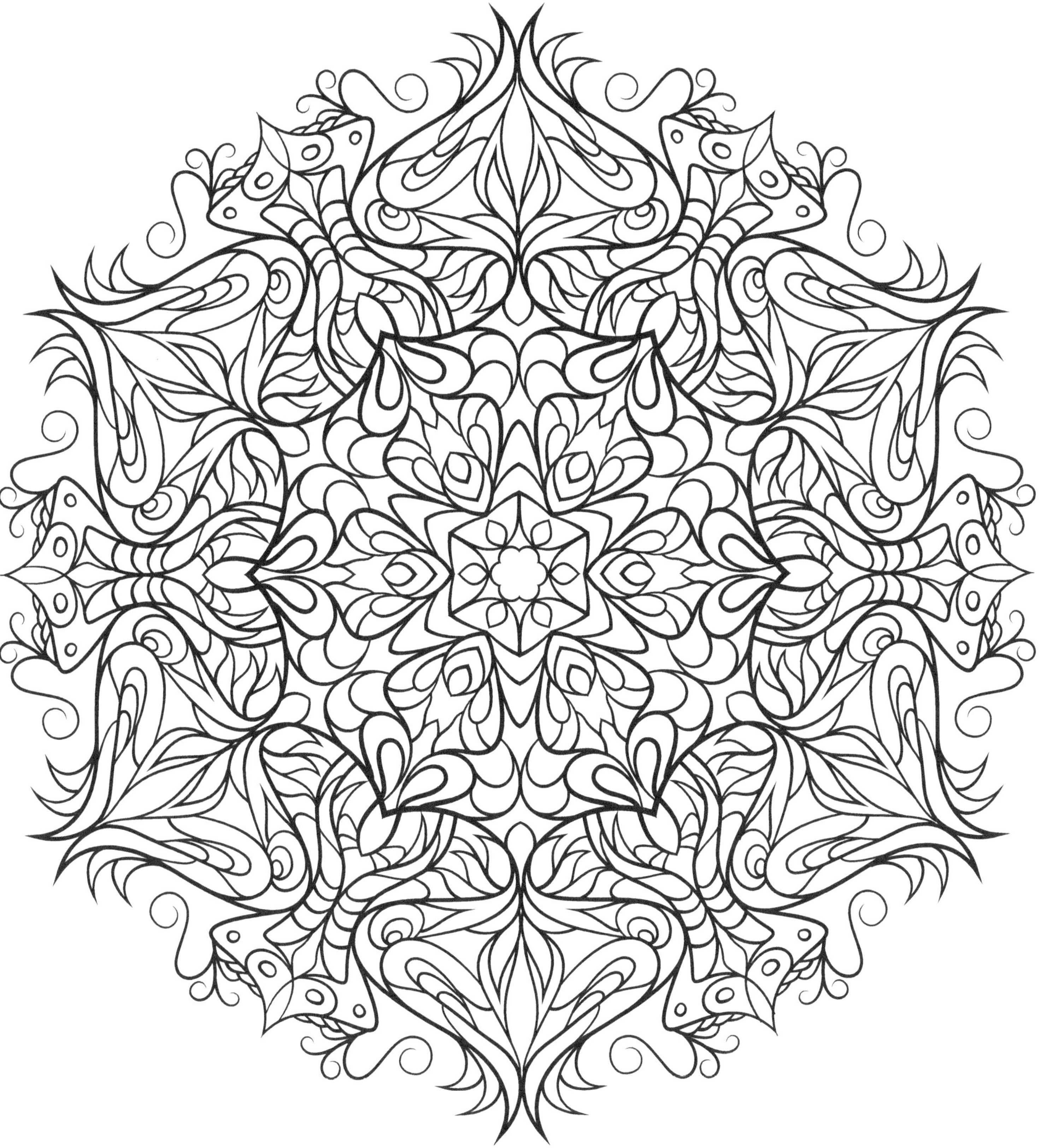

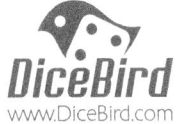

Poison

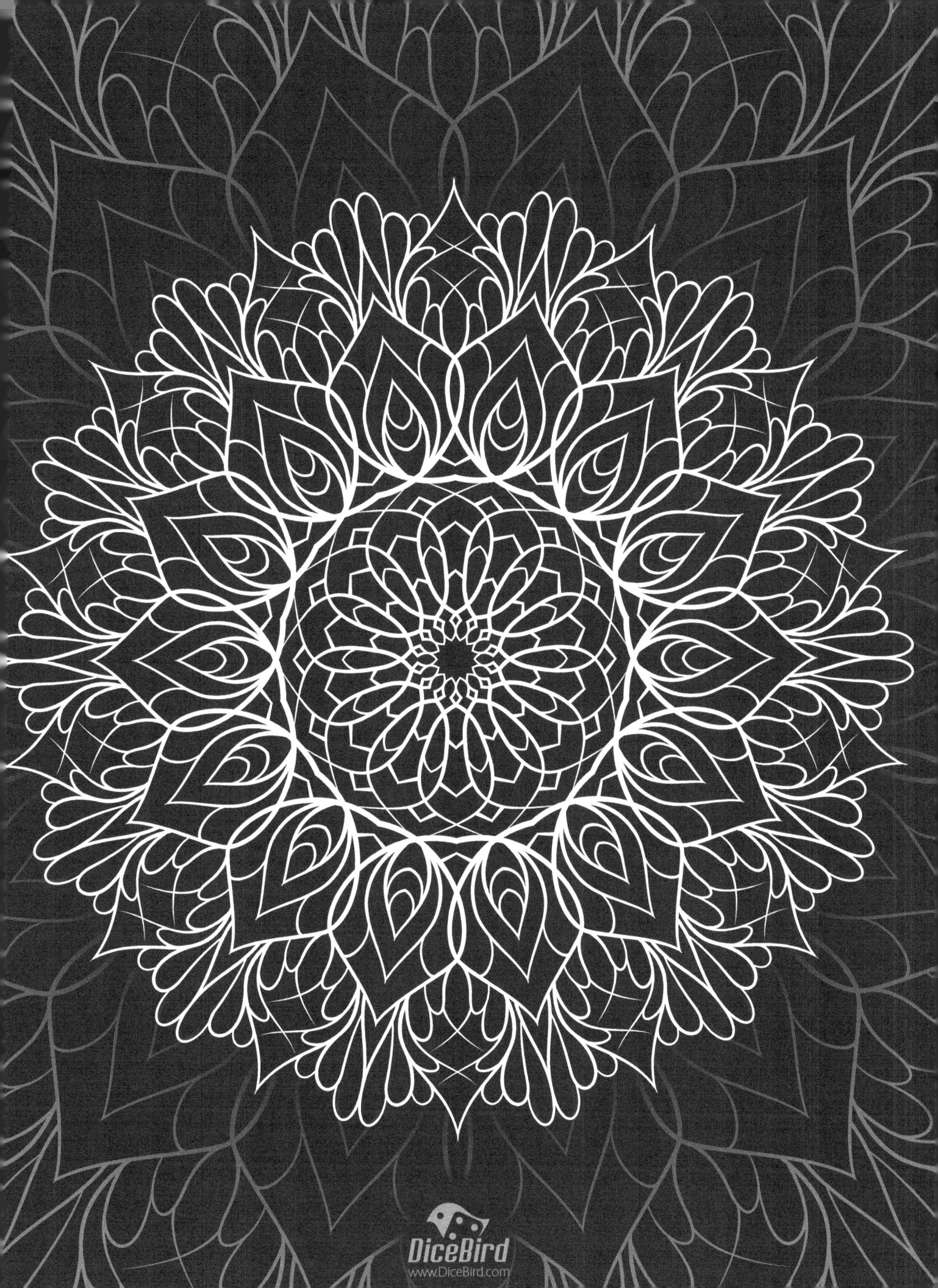

Life

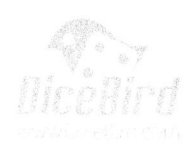

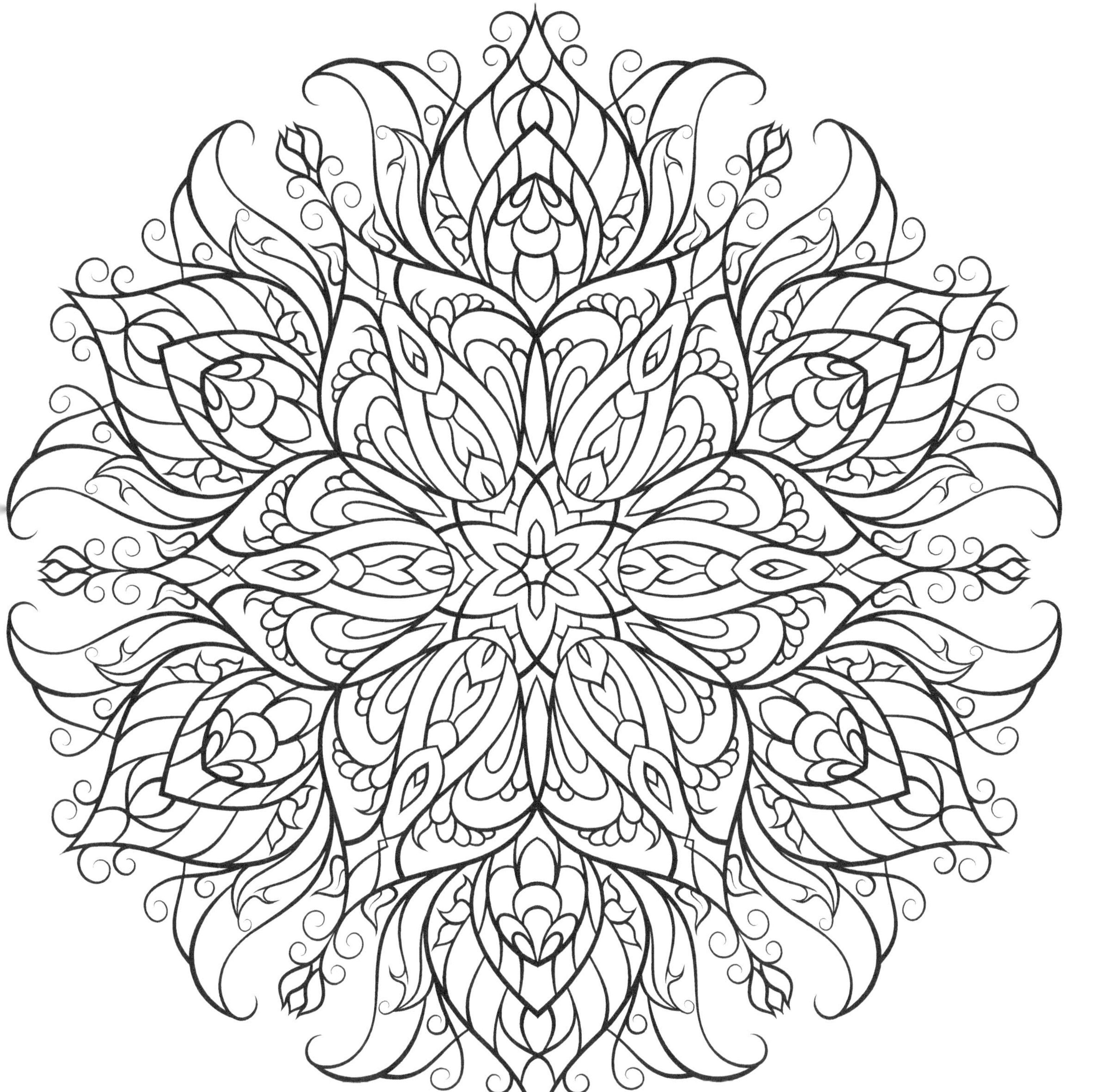

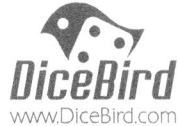

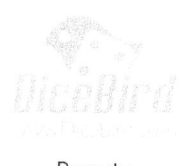

Beauty

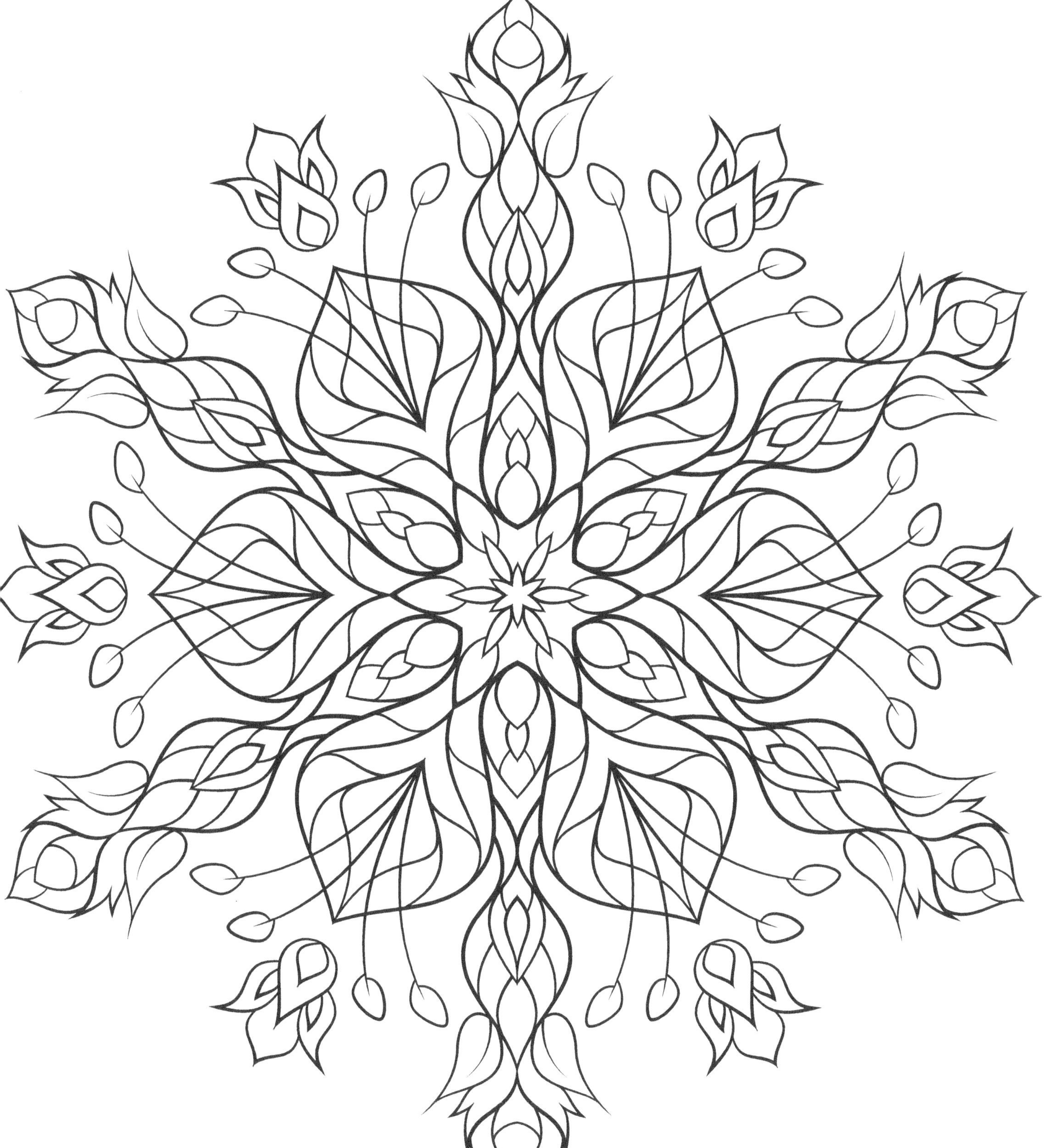

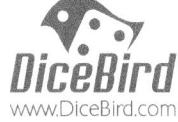

Peace

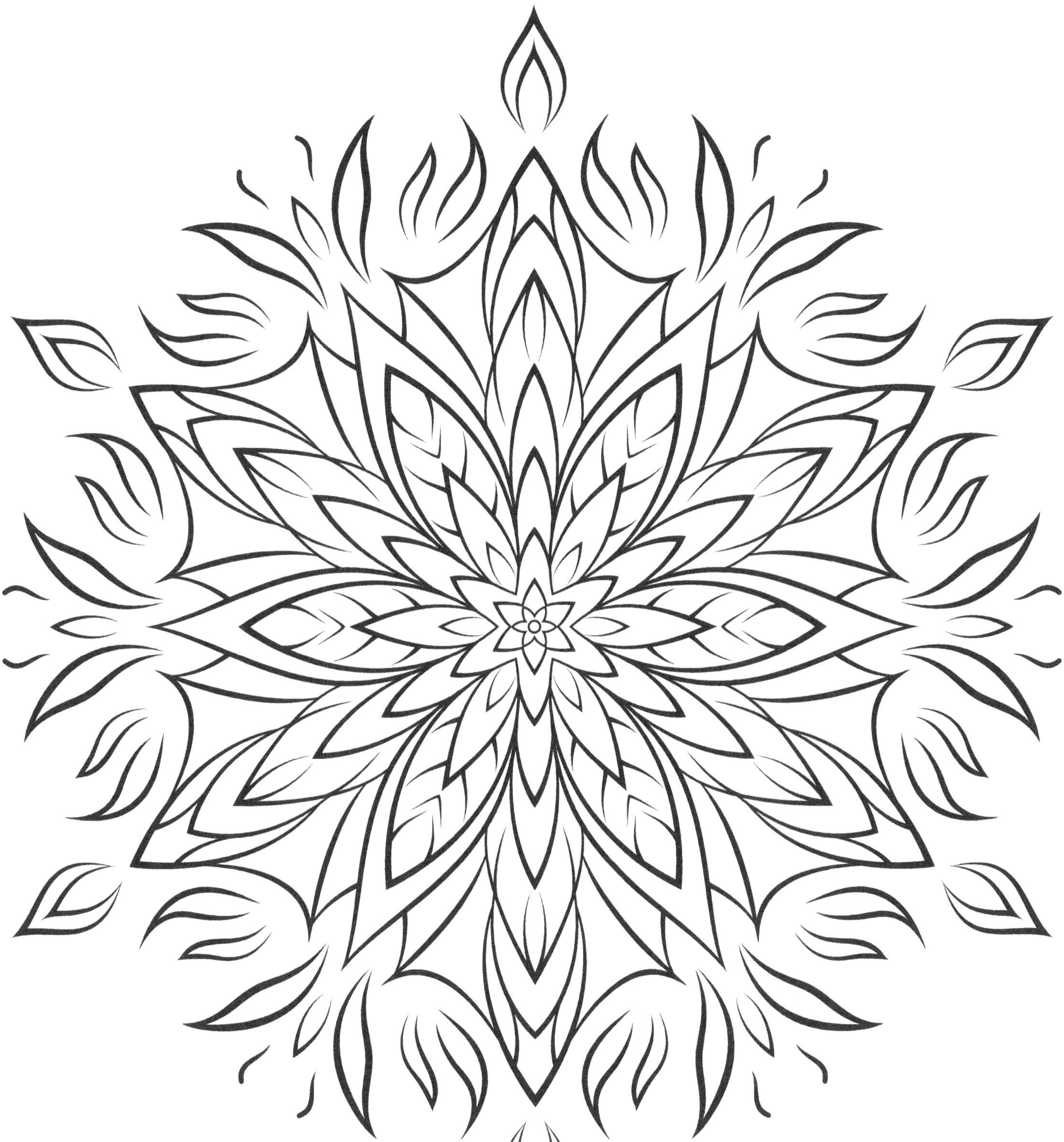

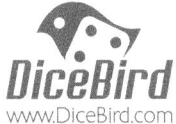

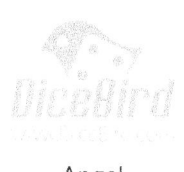

Angel

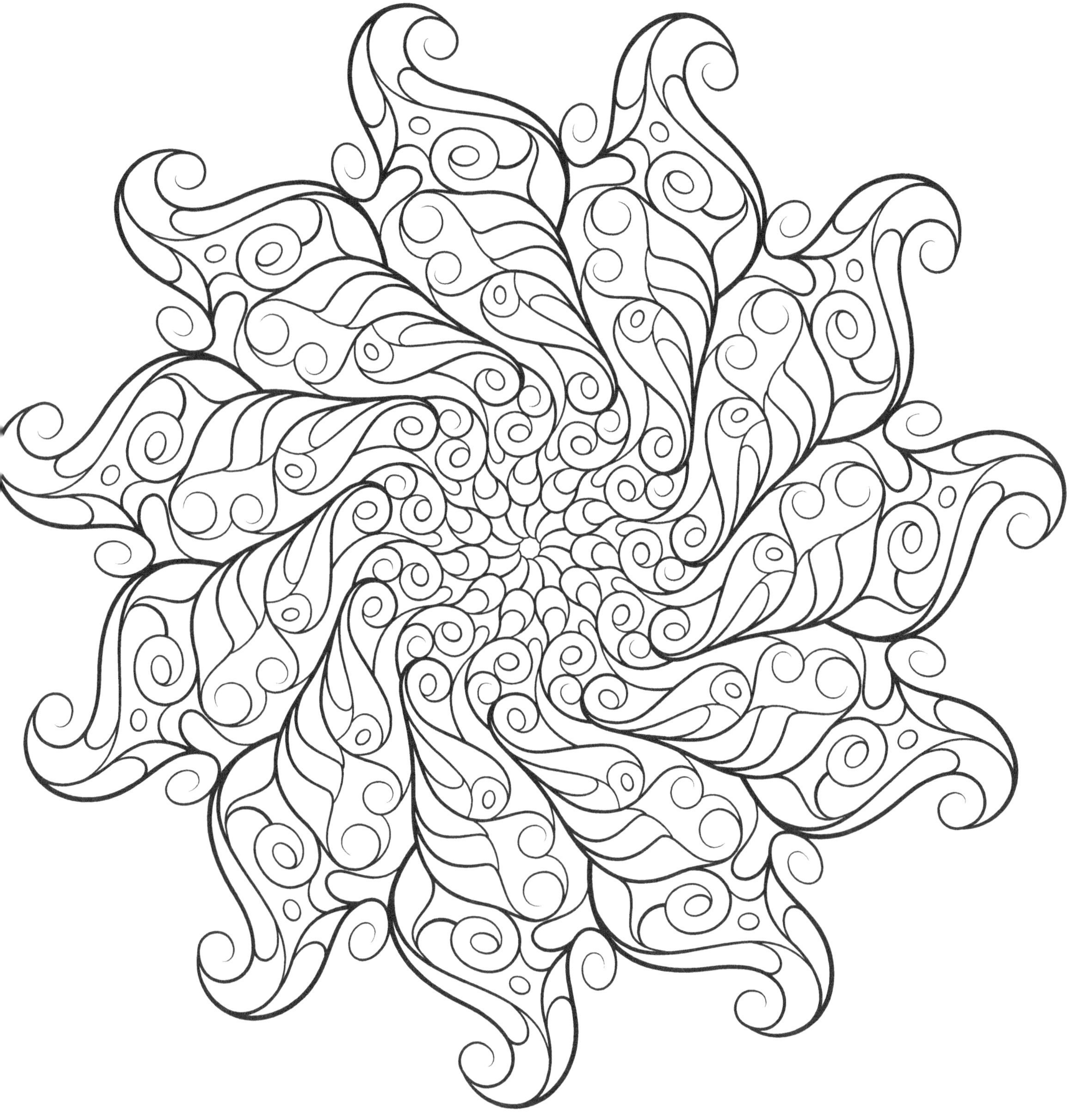

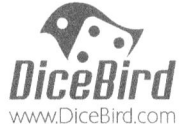

Curly

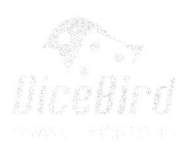